Bitcoin, Cryptocurrency and Blockchain

A Comprehensive Guide to Master the World of Crypto and Profit from the 2021 Bull Run!

Charles Swing & Masaru Nakamoto

Bitcoin and Cryptocurrency Trading

Discover the Trading Strategies for Beginners to Get Rich during the 2021 Bull Run - Learn the Basics of Trading and Money Management to Maximize Your Profits

misuse of the information in question by the reader will render any resulting actions solely under their purview. There are no scenarios in which the publisher or the original author of this work can be in any fashion deemed liable for any hardship or damages that may befall them after undertaking information described herein.

Additionally, the information in the following pages is intended only for informational purposes and should thus be thought of as universal. As befitting its nature, it is presented without assurance regarding its prolonged validity or interim quality. Trademarks that are mentioned are done without written consent and can in no way be considered an endorsement from the trademark holder.

Table of Contents

Bitcoin and Cryptocurrency Trading

Introduction

Bitcoin has taken the world by storm once again when it crossed $20,000 per BTC in December of last year.

A lot of people are trying to improvise themselves as professional traders and are losing a lot of money, only helping those who actually know what they are doing accumulate an incredible amount of wealth.

To join the club of the few traders that actually make it, you need the right strategies and the right mindset. Notice how we did not include a large initial capital. In fact, while having more money to trade with means having more fire power, it is not necessary to have thousands of dollars to be profitable and build wealth.

In fact, when we started trading cryptocurrencies we only had a few hundreds to put into the market, but that sum yielded us thousands and thousands of dollars.

In this book you are going to discover all the strategies that have allowed us to take our trading skills to the next level. If you apply them diligently we are sure you are going to see amazing results in a relative short period of time.

Please, stay away from all the shiny objects of the cryptocurrency world. Just choose one cryptocurrency pair, study it deeply and then milk it like a cash cow!

To your success!

Charles Swing and *Masaru Nakamoto*

Chapter 1 - Bitcoin

It is absolutely natural to start a cryptocurrency trading book by taking a look at the mother of all cryptocurrencies. Obviously, we are talking about bitcoin and the next few pages are going to lay out the foundations for the next chapters.

Bitcoin, represented with the symbol ฿, and with the ticker symbol BTC or XBT, is a cryptocurrency and a worldwide payment system created in 2009 by an anonymous inventor (or group of inventors), known under the pseudonym of Satoshi Nakamoto, who developed the idea from himself presented on the Internet at the end of 2008. By convention, if the term Bitcoin is used with a capital letter it refers to the technology and the network, while if the term bitcoin is used in lowercase it refers to the currency itself.

By financial experts, Bitcoin is not classified as a currency, but as a store of value that is currently very volatile. Unlike most traditional currencies, Bitcoin does not use a central entity or sophisticated financial mechanisms. In fact, its value is determined solely by the supply and demand ratio. It uses a database distributed among the nodes of the network that hold trace of transactions, but use cryptography to manage functional aspects, such as the generation of new money and the attribution of ownership of bitcoins. This technology is called "blockchain" and we will discuss more about it in the next chapter.

The Bitcoin network allows the pseudo-anonymous possession and transfer of coins. The data necessary to use one's bitcoins can be saved on one or more personal computers or electronic devices such as smartphones, digital "wallet", or kept with third parties that perform functions similar to a bank. The bitcoin wallet has an address identified by an alphanumeric code that has between 25 and 36 characters between numbers and letters. The address is the only data that needs to be communicated in order to receive a payment that will enjoy a certain degree of anonymity, but will at the same time be publicly and immutably visible on the blockchain forever. It is necessary to be very careful in transmitting the alphanumeric code as any errors do not allow the operation to be canceled and cause the loss of money. It is possible to receive payments more easily by scanning QR codes that represent the wallet address. In any case, bitcoins can be transferred over the Internet to anyone with a bitcoin address, no matter the distance between the two individuals. The peer-to-peer structure of the Bitcoin network and the lack of a central entity makes it impossible for any authority, government or company to block transfers, seize bitcoins without the possession of the relevant keys or devaluation due to the entry of new currency.

What most people don't know is that Bitcoin is one of the first implementations of a concept defined as cryptocurrency, first described in 1998 by Wei Dai on a mailing list that saw little to no interest.

A bit of price history

The first exchange rate was on October 5th, 2009 and set the value of one dollar at 1309 BTC.

Bitcoin reached $1,000 for the first time on November 27th, 2013. New historical records were reached on December 17th, 2017, reaching $20,000 per Bitcoin. The value then plummeted rapidly, dropping below $8,000 in February 2018 and stabilizing at around $6,000 for the rest of 2018. Since 2019, the value has fluctuated from a low of around $3,500 in January to over $40,000 in December 2020. On March 13th, 2021, after Tesla's purchase of $1.5b in BTC, it reached its highest historical value exceeding $ 61,000.

As you might understand by this quick look at Bitcoin's price history, it is a very volatile asset that gives a lot of opportunity to traders that can take advantage of big fluctuations in the market.

Bitcoin's tokenomics

The total value of the Bitcoin economy, calculated in December 2012 was about 140 million US dollars, in April 2013 1.4 billion US dollars, in November 2013, with an exchange rate of 1 bitcoin = 540 USD , the countervalue rose to more than 6 billion US dollars. The "psychological" threshold of $500 was first reached on Mt. Gox on November 17th, 2013 and just two days later, on the same exchange, the recorded value was $900 per Bitcoin. The $1,000 mark was first reached on November 27th of the same year; in December 2017 Bitcoin reached new all-time highs in the $20,000 area; In 2021 this value per unit of account was surpassed for the first time, this roughly coincided with the achievement of 1 trillion dollars of market cap (one-tenth of that of gold).

Once again, you can see the incredible volatility there is on this asset. You will soon discover that other cryptocurrencies are even more volatile.

Paying using Bitcoin

The bitcoin-based economy is still very small when compared to long-established economies, and the project is still in a beta release state; however, real goods and services such as used cars or software development contracts are already traded in bitcoin. Bitcoins are accepted for both online services and tangible goods.

There are now many entities, organizations and associations that accept bitcoin donations; among the many we can mention the Electronic Frontier Foundation, The Pirate Bay, the Free Software Foundation and also the Wikimedia Foundation.

Since November 2013, the University of Nicosia in Cyprus has accepted bitcoin as a means of payment for university fees. As of July 1st 2016, in the city of Zug, capital of one of the richest cantons in Switzerland, it is possible to pay for some public services in bitcoin, including healthcare and transport. Some merchants, using exchange sites, allow bitcoin to be exchanged for various currencies, including US dollars, euros, Russian rubles, and Japanese yen.

Anyone can check the list of bitcoin exchanges (written on the Blockchain) and observe the transactions in real time. Several services are already available to facilitate these operations. For instance, www.blockchain.com is a great resource to look at bitcoin's transactions.

Differences with legal tender currencies

Unlike other fiat currencies, bitcoins have a unique feature. In fact, no one can control their value due to the decentralized nature of the currency's creation method. In Bitcoin the amount of currency in circulation is limited a priori, moreover it is perfectly predictable and therefore known by all its users in advance. Circulating currency inflation cannot therefore be used by a central entity to redistribute wealth among users.

Transfers are defined as a change in ownership of the currency and are made without the need for an external entity to supervise the parties. This exchange method makes it impossible to cancel the transaction and therefore re-appropriate the coins that have changed ownership. The Bitcoin client transmits the transaction to its closest nodes, which verify its authenticity and the availability of funds and in turn retransmit it to the nodes to which they are connected.

The total number of bitcoins tends asymptotically to the limit of 21 million. The availability of new coins grows as a geometric series every 4 years; in 2013, half of the possible coins were generated and by the end of 2021 they will be more than three quarters. In this way, almost all coins will be generated in less than 32 years. As that date approaches and assuming that the demand for bitcoins will grow more than proportionally to their availability, bitcoins will likely suffer a deflation in value (i.e. an increase in real value) due to the scarcity of new money. In any case, bitcoins are divisible up to the eighth decimal place (with a total therefore of $2,1x1015$ units), allowing a complete adjustment of the value in a deflationary environment. According to the developers, in a bitcoin-scarce environment the nodes, instead of financing themselves by creating new bitcoins, will profit from their ability to collect transaction fees, thus competing on transaction costs and keeping them low.

In 2013, the virtual currency reached 21% of the total exchange operations of the Chinese currency.

Possible outcomes

Among the scenarios predicted for a possible Bitcoin bankruptcy, are the devaluation of the currency, a dwindling user base, or a frontal attack on the system by governments. However, it is not possible to ban all forms of digital money such as Bitcoin. The decentralization and anonymity that are intrinsically part of Bitcoin can be seen as a reaction to the legal proceedings against companies that worked in the field of electronic money such as e-gold and Liberty Dollar. This is because the system itself is in effect a collection of savings, heavily regulated in all countries of the world in a repressive sense. In an investigation by Danny O'Brien published in the Irish Times it is said that "When I show people the Bitcoin economy, they ask 'But is it legal?' and "Is this a scam?". I guess there are lawyers and economists who are trying to answer these not-so-simple questions. I suspect that the list of people who try to give this answer will soon be enriched with legislators".

The values of the currency are founded on the trust of its users. The management of bitcoin, and therefore its value and exchange rate, are entrusted to the free market and therefore to the forces of supply and demand.

Market developments and regulation

Some commentators raise doubts about the real technical possibility of blocking anonymous cryptocurrency exchanges on the internet. The restrictions would be motivated by the activity of criminal and terrorist organizations in anonymous and crypto exchanges, by the risk of the numerous and small savers who buy cryptocurrencies as a safe haven or to earn on price changes, by the instability created by the few large investors on the stock market.

The measures vary from the path of self-regulation of the sector with the creation of national registers of authorized operators, to the suspension of securities on the stock exchange, prohibition of anonymous transactions reserving them for those who have an authenticated bank account, to the blocking of credit cards.

Another issue is the ownership and control of money, and of the wealth exchanged in Bitcoin without passing through traditional banking investment channels. The cryptocurrency is issued by operators sometimes listed on the stock exchange, but who do not own the value introduced into the trading circuits, and who "are out of control" because they operate in a multinational context and are not in themselves influenced by the monetary policy instruments of the central banks (a rate hike, etc.). Properly, credit cards cannot be used by users to directly make purchases of goods sold in cryptocurrencies as is possible with a foreign currency: first the cryptocurrency must be purchased by depositing it on a virtual account, from which it is then possible to trade it.

If eBay intends to abandon PayPal from 2020, the well-known payment platform since 2016 has introduced the possibility of buying Bitcoin to buy goods in 40 countries, moving to a site that collects the most popular payment systems, while Amazon is negotiating with various banks to open Bitcoin checking accounts.

The limitations have primarily affected Bitcoin, which is the oldest cryptocurrency and among those with the highest frequency and volume transacted. On September 19th, 2017, the Chinese government blocked cryptocurrency exchanges in Shanghai and Beijing. Bitcoin calculates that in China 30% of the value of total exchanges is concentrated in the 1,200 cryptocurrencies surveyed, making it the main financial - and speculative - world center in this type of currency.

The investor risks the entire capital, but the financial gains through cryptocurrencies in China are not taxed, with only the obligation for US investors to declare more than $10,000 of capital gain.

On the same day, Japan was one of the first and few countries in the world to recognize the legitimacy of cryptocurrencies, introducing regulation and registering eleven traders in a register established at the stock exchange regulator, used by some companies as a benefit for their employees.
The news came just hours after a similar decision by the US SEC, which under federal law has the power to shut down illegal sites: the US and Japan are the most dynamic markets for electronics news and Internet commerce.

The Lloyd group and Bank of Scotland have blocked their customers from purchasing Bitcoin, following the American

Citigroup, Bank of America and JPMorgan, while the May government legislated on the matter, allowing free crypto trading in the UK.

The main Australian banks have "frozen" without warning the accounts of users and traders (with access to the stock exchange) denominated in cryptocurrencies, while the Government, without intervening, has eliminated double taxation with respect to national currencies.

Chapter 2 - Bitcoin and its Technology

While in the previous chapter we have talked about the economy behind Bitcoin, in the following pages we are going to discuss the fundamental technology that stands behind it and the other cryptocurrencies we are going to talk about later in this book.

In fact, understanding the technology is essential to become a profitable trader, as it directly affects the price of BTC and other crypto.

Bitcoin is a peer-to-peer implementation of Wei Dai's b-money proposition and Nick Szabo's Bitgold. The principles of the system are described in the "white paper" published by Satoshi Nakamoto.

The official client, Bitcoin Core, is a free software that derives directly from the code written by Satoshi Nakamoto to implement the communication protocol and the resulting peer-to-peer network.

Overview

Bitcoin relies on the transfer of currency between public accounts using public key cryptography. All transactions are public and stored in a distributed database which is used to confirm them and prevent the possibility of spending the same coin twice.

Property

Each user participating in the Bitcoin network owns a wallet that contains an arbitrary number of cryptographic key pairs. Public keys, or "bitcoin addresses", act as sending or receiving points for all payments. Possession of bitcoins implies that a user can only spend the bitcoins associated with a specific address. The corresponding private key is used to digitally sign each transaction making sure that only the user who owns that currency is authorized to pay. The network verifies the signature using the public key.

If the private key is lost, the Bitcoin network will not be able to recognize the ownership of the money in any other way. In fact, the relative sum of money will be unusable by anyone and, therefore, to be considered irretrievably lost. Cases of asset loss due to loss of the private key have already occurred in the first years of operation of the cryptocurrency. For example, in 2013 a user complained of the loss of 7,500 bitcoins, at the time worth 7.5 million dollars, for accidentally disposed of a hard drive that contained his private key.

Anonymity

The addresses contain no information about their owners and are generally anonymous. The addresses in readable form are random sequences of characters and digits with an average length of 33 characters, which always begin with 1, by 3 or by bc1, of the following form

1NAfBQUL4d2N7uu1iKxjwF8dESXTT3AKcq

Users can have an arbitrary number of Bitcoin addresses, and in fact it is possible to generate them at will without any limit as their generation costs little calculation time (equivalent to the generation of a public / private key pair) and does not require any contact with other nodes in the network. Creating a new key pair for each transaction helps maintain anonymity.

The algorithm used by Bitcoin to generate the keys is the Elliptic Curve Digital Signature Algorithm (ECDSA).

Transactions

Bitcoins contain their owner's public key (i.e. address). When a user A transfers money to user B he renounces his ownership by adding B's public key (his address) to the coins in question and signing them with his own private key. It then transmits these coins in a message, the "transaction", through the peer-to-peer network. The rest of the nodes validate the cryptographic signatures and the amount of digits involved before accepting it.

The blockchain and confirmations

To prevent the possibility of using the same coin multiple times, the network implements what Satoshi Nakamoto describes as a "peer-to-peer timestamp server", which assigns sequential identifiers to each of the transactions which are then enforced in the comparisons of modification attempts using the idea of a proof-of-work chain (shown in Bitcoin as "confirmations").

Each time a transaction is made, it starts in the "unconfirmed" state. It will only become "confirmed" when verified through a collectively managed timestamp list of all known transactions, called the blockchain.

In particular, each "generator" node collects all the unconfirmed transactions it knows in a candidate "block". It is a file which, among other things, contains a cryptographic hash of the previous valid block known to that node. It then tries to reproduce a hash of that block with certain characteristics, an effort that requires on average a definable amount of tests to be carried out. When a node finds such a solution it announces it to the rest of the network. The peers that receive the block check its validity before accepting it and then adding it to the chain.

When a transaction is admitted to a block for the first time, it receives a confirmation. Each time other blocks linked to it are created above that block, it receives another confirmation. When the block containing the transaction reaches six confirmations, i.e. six blocks linked to it are created, the Bitcoin client changes the status of the transaction from "not confirmed" to "confirmed". The reason behind this procedure is that with each confirmation of the transaction, that is, with each new block that is created above the block with the transaction itself, it becomes increasingly difficult and expensive to cancel the transaction. A hypothetical attacker, to cancel a transaction with a certain number of confirmations, would have to generate a parallel chain without the transaction he wants to cancel and composed of a number of blocks equal to or greater than the confirmations received by the transaction.

It follows that the block chain contains the history of all the movements of all the bitcoins generated starting from the address of their creator up to the current owner. So, if a user tries to reuse a coin that he has already spent, the network will reject the transaction as the sum will already be spent.

Nakamoto has designed the system in such a way that, although the database increases in size over time, it is possible to have a reduced version that covers only some transactions in detail, but which remains completely independently verifiable. For example, for a private user it might be interesting to have the block chain with only the transactions that concern them. Or, it may be desirable to purge from the database all transactions whose outgoing sums have already been used in other transactions, greatly decreasing their size. It is possible to do and resources like www.blockchain.com help people to dive deeper into this topic.

The creation of bitcoins

The Bitcoin network creates and distributes a certain amount of coins in a completely random manner approximately six times an hour to clients who actively participate in the network, i.e. who contribute through their own computing power to the management and security of the network. itself.

The business of generating bitcoin is often referred to as "mining", a term analogous to gold mining. The likelihood of a certain user receiving the coin reward depends on the computational power he adds to the network relative to the total computational power of the network.

Initially, the client itself took care of carrying out the calculations necessary for the extraction of bitcoins, using only the CPU. As the total computing power of the network increased and as a result of the competitive nature of the bitcoin creation process, this feature became expensive and was removed. Nowadays there are specialized programs which initially exploited the power of GPUs and FPGAs, and which now use dedicated hardware based on ASIC processors designed for this use.

Since the amount of operations on average required to successfully close a single block has become so high that it requires large amounts of resources in terms of electricity and computational power, most miners join in "teams" called mining pools where all the participants pool their resources, then dividing the blocks generated according to the contribution of each one.

The number of bitcoins created per block was initially 50 BTC (added to any costs of individual transactions). This quantity has been programmed to decrease over time according to a geometric progression with a halving of the prize approximately every 4 years (210,000 blocks). So dimensioned, this series means that in total about 21 million bitcoins will be created in the span of about 130 years, with 80% of these created in the first 10 years. The reward subsequently decreased to 25 BTC per block on November 28th, 2012, to 12.5 BTC per block on July 9th, 2016, to 6.25 BTC per block on May 11th, 2020. As the generation reward gradually decreases over time, the source of income for miners will shift from generating the coin to the transaction fees included in the blocks, until the day the reward ceases to be given: by then, transaction processing will be rewarded solely by the transaction fees themselves.

The amount of the commission can be freely set by who makes a transaction. However, from May 2013, with the update to version 0.8.2 of the official client, commissions below the threshold of 0.0001 BTC are considered non-standard and, consequently, the associated transactions risk never being confirmed. The higher the commission, the more likely it is to be included in the first block extracted, thus accelerating the first confirmation. Users therefore have an incentive to include such fees, because this means that the transaction will likely be processed more quickly. Furthermore, each miner has the freedom to choose which transactions to include in the block they are processing, which has a maximum size set by the protocol. Therefore, the miner will be encouraged to include transactions with higher fees first.

All the nodes in the network compete to be the first to find a solution to a cryptographic problem involving the candidate block, a problem that cannot be solved in any other way than by using bruteforce and therefore it essentially requires an enormous number of attempts. When a node finds a valid solution, it announces it to the rest of the network, simultaneously awarding the bitcoins in reward provided by the protocol. The nodes that receive the new block verify it and add it to their chain, starting the mining work again above the block as soon received.

From a technical point of view, the mining process is nothing more than an inverse hashing operation. In fact, determining a number (nonce) such that the SHA-256 hash of a set of data representing the block is less than a given threshold. This threshold, called "mining difficulty", is what determines the competitive nature of bitcoin mining. In fact, the more computing power is added to the bitcoin network, the more this parameter increases, consequently increasing the number of calculations on average needed to create a new block and thus increasing the cost of creating it, prompting nodes to improve the efficiency of their mining systems to maintain a positive economic balance. This parameter is updated approximately every 14 days, sizing itself so that a new block is generated on average every 10 minutes. The nodes that carry out the mining process are generally called miners.

Transaction costs

Considering that miners can independently decide which transactions to include in a block, those who want to send bitcoins will have to pay a transfer fee, of variable value, to encourage the choice of their transaction. Depending on the amount chosen to be paid as a transfer fee, the transfer will take place in more or less time. This mechanism constitutes an important incentive for miners, and will allow them to continue with their business even when the difficulty of generating bitcoins increases or the amount of reward per block decreases over time. Miners collect transaction fees associated with all transactions in their dedicated block.

Now that we have talked about the technological infrastructure behind the Bitcoin network, we can learn how to actually buy some bitcoins. This is the first step to start trading crypto, so pay close attention to the next chapter.

Bitcoin and Cryptocurrency Trading

Chapter 3 - How to Buy Bitcoin

As we have seen in previous chapters, bitcoin is an alternative online currency system, which serves as a digital store of value. Bitcoins are used both as an investment and as a payment method for goods and services, and it is appreciated by many because it eliminates intermediaries. Despite the growing popularity of this currency, many businesses still do not accept it and its usefulness as an investment is very dubious and potentially risky according to most people. Obviously, our opinion is much different.

Before starting to buy bitcoins, it is important to understand what they are, their advantages and disadvantages.

We have already said this in the first chapter, but repetition makes perfect. Bitcoin is a completely virtual currency, which allows users to exchange value for free, without relying on third parties (such as banks, credit cards or other financial institutions). Bitcoins are not regulated or controlled by a central authority such as the FED and all transactions take place in an online marketplace, where users are anonymous and almost completely untraceable.

The Bitcoin network allows people to instantly exchange money with any other person in the world, without having to create a merchant account, or rely on a bank or financial institution. Furthermore, money transfers don't require names, so the risk of identity theft is low.

Recently, the US agency responsible for combating money laundering announced new guidelines for virtual currencies. These rules will regulate bitcoin exchanges, but leave the rest of the Bitcoin economy intact for the time being. When you purchase bitcoin, you must consider the fact that the US federal law enforcement may conclude in the future that the Bitcoin network is a money laundering tool and may seek ways to dismantle it. While completely eliminating bitcoins is a real challenge, strict legislative regulation could greatly reduce the spread of the system and greatly limit the legitimacy of the currency.

Advantages and disadvantages of Bitcoin

This currency guarantees low fees, identity theft protection, payment fraud protection, and instant transactions. Let's look at them in more detail.

- **Low commissions**. Contrary to what happens with traditional financial systems, where the system itself (such as PayPal or a bank) is compensated with a commission, the Bitcoin network does not provide for any cost for users. The network is maintained by the miners, who are rewarded with new money.

- **Identity theft protection**. The use of bitcoins does not require your name or any other personal information, but simply an ID for the digital wallet (the medium used to send and receive bitcoins). Contrary to what happens with credit cards, where the broker has full access to your personal information and your account, Bitcoin users operate completely anonymously.

- **Fraud protection.** Since bitcoins are digital, they cannot be counterfeited and therefore being scammed becomes impossible. Furthermore, the transactions are not reversible, contrary to what happens with credit cards.

- **Instant transfers.** Historically, money transfers have often encountered delays, withholdings or other issues. The lack of a third party ensures that money can be transferred between people with ease and without the complexities, fees and delays associated with purchases made with different currencies.

However, it is not all sunshine and rainbows. With a traditional bank account, if an attacker makes a fraudulent transaction with your credit card or your bank goes bankrupt, there are laws designed to limit consumer losses. Unlike normal banks, the Bitcoin network does not have a security system to protect users from losing the currency. There is no intermediary entity that can reimburse you.

Keep in mind that the Bitcoin network is not immune to hacker attacks, and the average Bitcoin account is not entirely protected from attackers or free from security loopholes.

One study found that 18 out of 40 businesses that offered bitcoin exchange for other currencies closed and only 6 of them reimbursed their customers.

Exchange volatility is also a significant downside. This means that the price of Bitcoin in dollars fluctuates a lot. For example, in 2013, 1 bitcoin was worth about $13. It quickly climbed to $1200 and jumped to $19,000 in January 2018. For this reason, if you decide to buy Bitcoin it is important to keep your investment, otherwise you could lose a significant amount of countervalue.

The risk associated with investing in Bitcoin

One of the most popular uses of Bitcoin is investing, and this practice deserves special attention before continuing our journey in the world of cryptocurrency trading. The main risk of bitcoins is their volatility. Due to the very rapid fluctuations of the price, the risk of losing the investment is very high.

Furthermore, given that the value of bitcoins is determined by supply and demand, if this currency were to be regulated by any form of law, the number of users could decrease, theoretically rendering the currency worthless.

How to store Bitcoin

You have two options here. You can decide to store your bitcoins on an exchange or use a wallet. Let's take a look at the differences between these two methods.

Store your bitcoins on the internet

To purchase this currency, you must first create an electronic accumulation system. There are currently two ways to do this:

- **Deposit the keys of your bitcoins in an electronic wallet.** This is a file on your computer that you can put your money into, similar to a real wallet. You can create one by installing the Bitcoin client, the program that generates the currency. However, if your computer is attacked by a virus, a hacker, or if you lose the file, you could lose your bitcoins as well. Always backup your online wallet to an external hard drive to avoid losing your currency.

- **Deposit your bitcoins in a third party service.** You can also create an electronic wallet on third party sites, such as Coinbase or Binance, by saving the currency in their wallet. This system is simpler to set up, but it does mean entrusting your bitcoins to a third party. The sites mentioned are two of the largest and most reliable ones, but there are no guarantees as to their safety.

Create a paper wallet for your bitcoins

It is one of the most used and least expensive solutions to keep your currency safe. The wallet is small, compact and made with paper that has a code printed on it. One of the benefits is that your private keys are not stored in a digital environment, so they cannot be subjected to cyberattacks or hardware failures.

Many internet sites produce paper wallets for Bitcoins. They can generate a Bitcoin address for you and create an image that contains two QR codes. One is the public address that you can use to receive Bitcoin. The other is the private key, which you will use to spend the currency deposited in that address.

The images can be printed on a piece of paper that you can fold and take with you.

Use a physical wallet to deposit your bitcoins

Wallets of this type are very interesting. They are dedicated devices that can store private keys in electronic form and facilitate payments. They are usually small, compact and some are shaped like USB sticks.

- The Trezor wallet is mainly used by miners who wish to acquire large amounts of bitcoins, but who do not want to rely on third-party sites.
- The Ledger wallet works as a USB storage system for your bitcoins and uses smartcard security. It is one of the least expensive physical wallets on the market.

We advise you to choose a physical wallet to store your cryptocurrencies as it is the safest and easiest method available. Particularly, we recommend you the Ledger Nano S.

How to buy bitcoins

Getting bitcoins from an exchange service is the easiest way to acquire this currency. These services work like all traditional exchange services - just register and convert the currency of your choice into bitcoin. There are hundreds of sites that offer this possibility and the best solution depends on your geographic location. However, below you will find some of the more well-known services.

- **Coinbase**. This popular exchange and e-wallet service also allows you to exchange dollars, sterlings and euros for bitcoin. The company has a website and a mobile app to allow users to buy and trade bitcoins with ease. Coinbase is set to go public this year.

- **Binance**. This exchange service offers users the ability to deposit, send, receive and trade bitcoin and hundreds of other cryptocurrencies. We warmly advise you to use this exchange when you are going to trade crypto as it offers good liquidity and a huge variety of tokens.

- **Kraken**. This site offers an e-wallet, and the ability to deposit real currency into your account and convert it into bitcoin. It is one of the oldest exchanges on the market and the one used by many early adopters.

Some exchange services also allow you to trade bitcoins. Others function as electronic wallets with limited buying and selling possibilities. Most of them keep amounts of real or digital money for you, just like regular bank accounts. They are a good option if you want to do bitcoin trades frequently and don't care about total anonymity. In fact, to register to these exchanges you will have to complete the KYC process.

When you sign up for an exchange service, you must provide your personal information to create an account. The laws of almost all states require that all entities, whether private or legal, using a Bitcoin exchange service meet the anti-money laundering requirements.
Even if you are asked to prove your identity, exchange services and e-wallets do not offer the same level of protection as banks. You are not protected from hackers and no refunds will be given if the site fails.

Once you have created a profile on an exchange service, you need to link it to an existing bank account and set up money transfers between the two. Usually you will have to do this with a wire transfer and you will have to pay a small commission.

Some foreign exchange services allow you to make in-person deposits into a bank account.

If you are asked to link a bank account to the exchange service account in order to use it, you will likely only be able to provide information from banks operating in the country where the service is based. Some services allow you to send money to overseas accounts, but the fees are much higher and currency exchanges may be delayed.

Our advice for you is to get accustomed to the use of different exchanges, as they are an important building block when it comes to investing and trading cryptocurrencies.

In the next few pages we are going to tell you the old method people used to get bitcoins, when exchanges were not as popular as these days. We are going to do this just for entertainment purposes and to give you a bit of historical background. We do not endorse this method in any way and we warmly advise you to use an exchange like Coinbase, Binance or Kraken.

How NOT to buy bitcoin

People used to look for vendors on LocalBitcoins. This was the most frequently used site for in-person exchanges between local sellers. You could arrange a meeting and negotiate the price of the virtual currency. The site also offered protection for both parties thanks to a rudimental escrow system.

Once they found a seller, people used to negotiate the price before the meeting. Depending on the seller, you had to pay a 5-10% surcharge for in-person transactions. You should have also asked the seller if they prefered to be paid in cash or with an online payment service. Some sellers accepted payments via PayPal, although most wanted non-reversible cash transactions.

A reputable seller would always negotiate the price with you before the meeting. Many also didn't wait too long to finalize the sale once an agreement was found, so as to avoid problems in the event of sudden fluctuations in the price of the asset.

After you agreed on the price, people used to meet the seller in a public place frequented by many people. You should have taken all possible precautions, especially if you carried the necessary cash with you.

You would have made sure you had access to your Bitcoin wallet with your smartphone, tablet or laptop. You needed an internet connection to confirm the success of the transaction. Finally, you had to always check that the bitcoins had been transferred to your account before paying the seller.

As you can see, this was a method that required one aspect that is fundamental for the average bitcoin user: trust. In fact, when you agreed to meet someone in person to exchange bitcoins with them, you basically had to trust this other person. Luckily, nowadays there are incredibly good exchanges that allow us to put our faith in them rather than in an unknown person. Of course, they are still an intermediary, but if you stick to the most famous ones you should have no problems. In fact, at the present moment, companies like Coinbase and Binance are heavily regulated and have to follow strict rules to operate, making them safe for the end user.

Chapter 4 - An introduction to Ethereum

Ethereum is the second cryptocurrency you must know and understand before starting trading crypto. In fact, as you are going to learn in the next few pages, a lot of crypto projects rely on the Ethereum blockchain for their existence.

Ethereum is a decentralized Web 3.0 platform for peer-to-peer creation and publication of smart contracts created in a Turing-complete programming language.

Ethereum had a stable value of around 10 dollars until 2017, the year in which it had a very strong increase in value, reaching a peak of 1,261 dollars on January 12th, 2018, and then falling again, with peaks in April 2018 (around 700 dollars), June 2019 (about $300), February 2020 (about $200) and December 2020 (about $600), rising in 2021 with a peak of over $2,000.

Features

In order to run on the peer-to-peer network, Ethereum contracts "pay" for the use of its computational power through a unit of account, called Ether, which therefore acts as both cryptocurrency and fuel. In other words, unlike many other cryptocurrencies, Ethereum is not just a network for exchanging monetary value, but a network for running Ethereum-based contracts. These contracts can be safely used to perform a large number of operations: electoral systems, domain name registration, financial markets, crowdfunding platforms, intellectual property, and many others.

The platform was first mentioned by Vitalik Buterin in Bitcoin Magazine, of which he himself is co-founder with Joseph Lubin, in early 2013. It was subsequently conceptualized in Buterin's own White Paper and formalized by Gavin Wood in the so-called Yellow Paper, at the beginning of 2014. The release of the first "live" version of the platform (the so-called Frontier version) took place on July 30th 2015.

Ethereum is part of a group of so-called "next generation" (or "2.0") blockchain platforms.

As with other cryptocurrencies, the validity of each Ether is guaranteed by a blockchain, which is an ever-growing list of records, called blocks, which are linked together and protected by cryptography. By definition, the blockchain itself is resistant to data modification. It is an open, distributed, accounting ledger that records transactions between two parties in an efficient and permanently verifiable manner.

Unlike Bitcoin, Ethereum operates using accounts and balances according to so-called state transitions, which are not based on unspent transaction outputs (UTXOs), but on the current balances (called states) of all accounts, as well as to some additional data. The information relating to the state is not stored in the blockchain, but is stored in its own Merkle tree. A Merkel tree is a binary tree in which each node is the father of two children nodes and its hash is given recursively by the concatenation of the hashes of the two associated blocks, according to the following scheme:

$$\{ \backslash\ displaystyle\ hash\_\ \{0\} = hash\ (hash\_\ \{0\text{-}0\} + hash\_\ \{0\text{-}1\})\}$$
$$\{ \backslash\ displaystyle\ hash\_\ \{0\} = hash\ (hash\_\ \{0\text{-}0\} + hash\_\ \{0\text{-}1\})\}$$

A cryptocurrency wallet stores public and private "keys" or "addresses" that can be used to receive or spend Ether.

As we have seen, private (deterministic) keys can be generated using the Bitcoin protocol called BIT32, starting from a sequence of 12 or 18 words that is stored in the Bitcoin wallet, from which the level 0 master private key is obtained and, downwards, those of the following levels. For each private key, the Bitcoin address associated with its level is generated.

On the contrary, in Ethereum, this procedure is not required, since it cannot work in a UTXO scheme: through the private key it is possible to write to the blockchain, effectively concluding an Ether transaction.

To route the Ether to an account, you need to have the computed hash of its public key, which is computed with the Keccak-256 encryption algorithm. Ether accounts are not nominative, they do not uniquely identify the beneficiary, but rather one or more specific addresses.

Ether

Ether is a critical component to the functioning of Ethereum, because it provides a ledger for transactions. It is used to pay for gas, a calculation unit for transactions and other state transitions. It is indicated with the ETH transaction icon (ticker symbol) and the Greek capital letter Ξ as the currency symbol, so that it can be traded in the electronic markets denominated in cryptocurrencies, i.e. pay transaction fees and additional services to the Ethereum network.

Addresses

The addresses of the Ethereum network begin and are identified by the prefix "0x", common for base 16 numbers, followed by the rightmost 20 bytes (byte order) of the Keccak-256 hash of the ECDSA public key where the curve used it is the so-called secp256k1, the same as Bitcoin. Since in base 16 two digits correspond to one byte, Ethereum addresses contain 40 hexadecimal digits (the standard prefix "0x", which is the invariant part, is not memorized, but "re-entered" from time to time). An example of an Ethereum address is the following.

0xb794F5eA0ba39494cE839613fffBA74279579268.

The contract addresses are in the same format, but are determined by the sender and the nonce, a scalar equal to the transaction number sent by the sender (contract creation). In other words, user accounts are indistinguishable from contract-accounts, which are associated with a single address for each and no blockchain data. A user, on the other hand, can have multiple levels of private key, from which as many Ethereum addresses are generated.

Any valid Keccak-256 hash entered in the described format is valid, even if it does not correspond to an account with a private key or to a contract. Unlike Ethereum, Bitcoin uses base58check to make sure addresses are spelled correctly.

The development

The development of Ethereum began in December 2013, and the first versions of the Go language and C ++ language software were released in early February 2014. Since then, several successive versions have been published, which have included the development of three programming languages specially created for writing smart contracts. They are the following.

- Serpent (inspired by the Python language)
- Mutan (inspired by the Go language)
- LLL (inspired by the language of Lisp programming)

To fund the development work, Ethereum launched a pre-sale public offering of Ether. The public offering lasted 42 days and totaled the collection of 31,591 Bitcoins, equal (at the exchange rate of September 2nd, 2014) to approximately 18.4 million US dollars, or 60,102.216 ETH.

Proof of Concept number 5 was released on GitHub on July 22nd, 2014, at the same time as the pre-sale launch of Ether, and included numerous changes from the previous Proof of Concept. For the first time the two clients, one written in C ++ and another in Go, have begun to interact perfectly and work on the same Blockchain. In August 2014, a client written in Python was added to the list of available platforms.

With Proof of Concept number 7, Solidity was launched, a hybrid programming language, inspired by JavaScript / C ++, containing numerous syntactic enrichments in order to be compatible and versatile for the compilation of smart contracts on Ethereum. Block times have been reduced from 60 seconds to 12 seconds, using a new GHOST-based protocol.

In 2015, Ethereum began using pre-sale fundraising to expand its operations, starting with the foundation based in Zug, Switzerland and with development teams in London, Berlin and Amsterdam. The beta version with a working network and in which mining gives rewards in real Ether, called Frontier, was released on July 30th, 2015. In addition to this, in July 2015 a bug research program was launched and is still open to the developer community.

Ethereum is an open source project, and any developer can contribute to the source code.

Ethereum's currency unit of account is called Ether and is abbreviated to the symbol ETH. Ether is divided into subunits of account called finney, szabo, shannon, babbage, lovelace, and wei, respectively in honor of Hal Finney, Nick Szabo, Claude Shannon, Charles Babbage, Ada Lovelace and Wei Dai, more or less known personalities in the world of cryptography, programming and cryptocurrencies.

A few quick words on smart contracts

Before concluding this chapter, we feel it is important to spend a few words on smart contracts. In fact, as you know by now, most cryptocurrencies are nothing more than a smart contract running on Ethereum. Therefore, we believe it is important to have at least a wide understanding of what a smart contract is before trying to profit from it.

Smart contracts are IT protocols that facilitate, verify, or enforce the negotiation or execution of a contract, sometimes allowing the partial or total exclusion of a contractual clause.

Smart contracts usually also have a user interface and often simulate the logic of contractual clauses.

It is important to underline that the above definition is somehow attributable to Nick Szabo. However, in current industrial practice by smart contract we mean a program that is executed on the validating nodes of a blockchain and whose result, which generally corresponds to a change of state of the blockchain itself, represents a transaction on which the validating nodes must find a consensus. The consensus algorithm can possibly be of the proof-of-work or proof-of-stake type or any other type that guarantees the integrity of the change of status and compliance with the rules of the protocol.

This meaning of smart contract is not exactly that of a contract, but rather that of a program whose execution and results are guaranteed by the properties of a public blockchain. This meaning derives from the choice of the Ethereum project to name this code running as a smart contract.

Advocates of smart contracts argue that many types of contract clauses can therefore be made partially or fully automated, self-fulfilling, or both. Smart contracts aspire to ensure greater security than existing contracts and to reduce transaction costs associated with bargaining.

Examples

Intellectual property rights management schemes are smart contracts for copyright licensing, as are financial encryption schemes for financial contracts. The eligibility check schemes, token bucket algorithms, and other quality of service mechanisms help facilitate agreements on the level of the services. Some P2P networks need mechanisms to ensure that outsiders can contribute remotely, and use resources, without requiring oversight of legal contracts. Two examples of such protocols are the computer data storage trading protocol in flŭd backup and the Mojo Nation filesharing auction. The cryptographic authentication of one part of the product, performed by another, was used in place of a contract between the producer and the consumer, to verify binding conditions.

As you might understand by now, smart contracts and blockchain are two very complicated topics. Luckily for you, you do not need to know every little detail of these topics to be a profitable trader. However, we felt it was important to give you an introductory description of this incredibly sophisticated and futuristic world.

Now it is time to truly begin our journey in the world of cryptocurrency trading.

Charles Swing & Masaru Nakamoto

Chapter 5 - Setting Up your Trading Account on Binance

The cryptocurrency exchange we recommend you is called Binance. In this chapter we are going to take a look at the account creation process. It is pretty straightforward and you can follow us along.

Opening an account on Binance.com the famous exchange to buy and sell cryptocurrencies is extremely simple. First of all, you need to have the following tools.

- PC, Desktop, Laptop, smartphone or Tablet;
- An internet connection;
- A valid document (identity card, passport, driving license);
- A valid email address;
- Personal data, address, tax code and residence;
- An active credit card or an active bank account;

Once you have the tools listed above, you can create a new account through the following steps.

- Go to the Binance.com platform and click on Register;
- Insert a valid email and a password;
- Click on "Create account" and the form to verify the email address will appear;
- Now you need to check the inbox of the email entered and open the email sent to you by Binance.com;
- Enter the code received by email on the screen and activate your account;

Once the code has been entered, the screen will appear to deposit funds such as Dollars (Fiat currency) and cryptocurrencies or buy cryptocurrencies with a credit card. You can click on the top right on "continue to the dashboard".

At this point, you can make the access to your account more secure by activating the "2FA" verification with Google Autenthicator or via text message.

We prefer the 2-factor verification of Google Authenticator (Android, Apple), as your phone number can be stolen. You just need to install the application on your smartphone and follow the instructions on the screen.

Once the 2-factor verification is activated, you can access your account much more safely.

At this point, the account is not active yet. In fact, in order to activate it you must verify your identity by sending a photo of a real and unexpired document in the "identification" section of your account.

Once the document has been verified, you can move on to the transfer of funds or directly to the purchase of cryptocurrencies in the "Buy Crypto" section.
You can choose between different methods to deposit your funds. We warmly advise you to use direct deposits, as they have the lowest fees on the market.

Chapter 6 - Setting Up your Coinbase Account

In the previous chapter we have seen how to set up a Binance account. In the next few pages we are going to take a look at how to register on Coinbase. We feel that every crypto trader must have a Coinbase account, as it is one of the safest exchanges that you can use to trade cryptocurrencies.

Why is one exchange not enough? Because the world of crypto moves extremely fast and being able to trade coins from different exchanges is extremely valuable during wild periods in the market. Furthermore, some coins that are listed on Binance are not listed on Coinbase and vice versa. Therefore, by having two accounts you get more exposure to the entirety of the market.

With a Coinbase wallet you can deposit fiat currencies from your bank account or credit card and have them credited to your Coinbase account. You can then use them to buy the cryptocurrencies available on the exchange.

The earnings from your trades can be transferred to your bank account. Furthermore, through the Coinbase smartphone app you can pay in bitcoin in stores that accept this form of payment.

Open your Coinbase account

Before opening your Coinbase account, you need the following things.

- an identity document with a photo;
- a computer with a webcam, a scanner or a Smartphone, to acquire the images of the document.

From your computer, open the web page https://www.coinbase.com/ and click on "Start Here".

Follow the registration procedure and create your Coinbase wallet. Proceed to the end and then click on "Create account".

The next page notifies you of the sending of an email that will arrive in the email box you provided during registration. You must verify the email address. At this point Coinbase will ask you for your telephone number in order to make transactions safer. Remember the 2-factor authentication on Binance? Here is the same process. Specify the number of your smartphone, and click on "send code" to receive a seven-digit code via SMS. Enter the code on your computer and click on "confirm".

Add a payment method

For a Coinbase wallet to be fully operational, you need to allow Coinbase to verify your identity and then add a payment method. To continue this process, click on "Complete your Account".

As soon as the "Verification of identity document required" page opens, select the option you prefer based on the photo document you decide to provide. Upload the document images after scanning them with your smartphone or scanner.

Once this is done, click on the "Verification completion" button. Identity verification takes a few minutes and after it is completed you will be redirected to the Coinbase login page. Enter your credentials and click on "Login".

Finally, to complete your account, you need to add a payment method. To do this, just click on "Complete your account". You can choose between two options:

- "Wire account", allows you to send and receive using wire transfers.
- "Visa and MasterCard Credit/debit card", more agile, especially in the case of a debit card, from where you can constantly check the amount of the card balance.

Other payment methods can also be chosen at a later time, but we encourage you to stick with wire transfers as they require less fees.

Bitcoin and Cryptocurrency Trading

Chapter 7 - Advantages of Cryptocurrency Trading

In this chapter we are going to discuss the advantages of cryptocurrency trading over other asset classes.

Volatility

Although the cryptocurrency market is relatively young, it has already experienced periods of high volatility, often due to short-term speculative movements. For example, between October 2017 and October 2018, the price of bitcoin rose as high as $19378, and then dropped dramatically to $5851. Making a comparison with the price trends of other cryptocurrencies, we can see how these have remained more stable, even if the launch of new technological tools has always attracted the interest of speculators.

Volatility is in fact one of the characteristics that makes the market more attractive to traders. Rapid intraday price movements offer a range of opportunities for traders to open long and short positions in the markets, but, at the same time, amplify the potential risks of the trades. Therefore, if you decide to explore the cryptocurrency market, make sure you have done all the necessary research and developed an effective risk management strategy.

Trading hours

The cryptocurrency market is available 24 hours a day, seven days a week, because it doesn't have a central entity that manages the markets. Transactions with cryptocurrencies can be made between two parties in markets on a global scale. However, periods of inactivity may also occur when markets need infrastructure upgrades, known as 'forks'.

Greater liquidity

Liquidity is the measure of the speed of converting a cryptocurrency into cash, without affecting the market price. It is also important because it provides better prices, improves transaction timing and accuracy to facilitate the technical analysis of the markets.

In general, the cryptocurrency market is considered illiquid, because transactions are dispersed across multiple trading venues, so even small trading operations can have a major impact on market prices. This partly explains why cryptocurrency markets are so volatile.

However, when trading cryptocurrencies using Coinbase or Binance, you will benefit from greater liquidity as they provide prices from multiple trading venues on your behalf. This means that your trades can be executed quickly and at lower prices.

Possibility to go long or short

When you buy a cryptocurrency as an investment, you are buying the asset in advance with the aim of seeing an increase in its value. When trading the price of a cryptocurrency, you are looking to make a profit from both the rising and falling markets. When you open a short position (from which the expressions 'go short', 'short selling' or 'sell short' derive), you are hoping to see the price go lower.

Let's assume, for example, that you want to open a short position on Binance on the price of the cryptocurrency EHT because you think the market will lose value. If your prediction turns out to be correct and therefore ETH depreciates against the US dollar, you would make a profit. However, if the value of ETH appreciates against the US dollar, your position would close at a loss.

Hedging
Trading cryptocurrency also offers some tax advantages. However when trading cryptocurrencies you will always have to pay a capital gains tax. Crypto still allows you to hedge, because you can offset losses with profits.

Financial leverage
Being leveraged products, cryptocurrencies allow you to trade on margin, i.e. the deposit of a sum of money that corresponds to a small fraction of the total value of the trading operation. In

other words, with leverage you get greater exposure to the chosen cryptocurrency by investing only a small portion of your capital.

The profit or loss you may experience from your cryptocurrency trading operations will reflect the total position value at the time the market closes, which is why trading on margin offers the possibility of making greater profits through a relatively modest investment. As with profits, however, leverage can expose you to the risk of amplifying your losses as well, which may even exceed your initial deposit. This is why it is crucial, before undertaking a trade using leverage, to consider the total cost of the position you intend to open, also considering the leverage effect.

Before starting trading cryptocurrencies, it is also essential to study and apply an effective risk management strategy, with the inclusion of appropriate stops and limits.

The next chapter is going to tell you more about money management when trading cryptocurrencies.

Bitcoin and Cryptocurrency Trading

<u>Chapter 8 - Money Management Strategies</u>

Money management, or capital management, is a fundamental step that every trader must take before starting to operate with online trading. Regardless of the type of asset one is willing to trade, money management can never be lacking.

Capital management is in fact a fundamental part of any long-term trading strategy. Knowing how to manage your capital means avoiding unpleasant losses, as well as having better risk management.

Each money management strategy is different. In fact, a lot depends on the type of trading you want to do, but also on the initial economic availability. Not to mention your skill and professionalism. Experienced traders will be able to afford to risk more, since they know the logic of the markets well.

However, there are some fundamental points at the basis of all money management techniques for online trading. Here are the ones that are usually included in every successful and reliable trading strategy.

- You need to start trading cryptocurrencies with adequate capital for the type of trading chosen;

- For each operation it is necessary to set a certain amount to trade also taking into account the available capital (usually 2-3% is chosen for each operation);

- Always use available risk management tools, such as Stop Loss and Take Profit;

- Identify the maximum risk for your portfolio, also known as the drawdown;

- Always follow a reliable and tested trading strategy, valid for the type of trading you want to do.

- Focus on one operation at a time, without relating them (to avoid unnecessary psychological stress that could have repercussions on capital management);

- Set achievable earnings goals (no ideas like "doubling your capital in just a month or two");

- Decide your intensity of trading (how many operations to do per day / week).

Every money management plan for cryptocurrencies online trading complies with at least all of these rules listed above. We must not underestimate any of the rules mentioned above, otherwise the risk of suffering a loss will be just around the corner.

Money management example to avoid losses
Theory and practice are two different stories, we all know this. In the case of cryptocurrency trading, there is a lot of money that risks being lost forever if the rules of money management

are not strictly applied. Below we want to show you the importance of choosing in advance a fixed amount to invest for each individual transaction.

There are many traders who religiously follow the rule of not risking more than 2-3% of their capital on each operation. Even if there are professional traders who go up to 5%, they are aware that they will take greater risks. The reason this rule exists is very simple.

You must avoid burning all your capital with a few wrong operations. For example, if we have a capital of $10,000 and we decide to invest $3,000 on a single operation, we expose 30% of our capital. It would be enough to open 3 operations in one day to have invested 90% of the capital.

The result is that too much risk would be taken. Earning in the long term with cryptocurrency trading requires excellent risk management. But maybe you are still skeptical.

After all, if you have never traded crypto before or if you have just started, it is normal to immediately "not believe" everything you read. You may think that investing only 2-3% is really too little, and the gains you could make with those figures are minimal.

Therefore, if you still have doubts about the (fundamental) rule of 2-3% to invest on each operation, we will show you its importance with a practical example. After all, numbers can't lie right? In the example table below you can see what we are talking about.

Trade	Total	2%risk	Trade	Total	10% risk
N°	Balance	$ per trade	N°	Balance	$ per trade

Bitcoin and Cryptocurrency Trading

1	$20,000	$400	1	$20,000	$2,000
2	$19,600	$392	2	$18,000	$1,800
3	$19,208	$384	3	$16,200	$1,620
4	$18,824	$376	4	$14,580	$1,458
5	$18,447	$369	5	$13,122	$1,312
6	$18,078	$362	6	$11,810	$1,181
7	$17,717	$354	7	$10,629	$1,063
8	$17,363	$347	8	$9,566	$957

9	$17,015	$340	9	$8,609	$861
10	$16,675	$333	10	$7,748	$775
11	$16,341	$327	11	$6,974	$697
12	$16,015	$320	12	$6,276	$628
13	$15,694	$314	13	$5,649	$565
14	$15,380	$308	14	$5,084	$508
15	$15,073	$301	15	$4,575	$458
16	$14,771	$295	16	$4,118	$412

17	$14,476	$290	17	$3,706	$371
18	$14,186	$284	18	$3,335	$334
19	$13,903	$278	19	$3,002	$300

We start trading with a whopping $20,000.

- On the one hand we choose to respect the 2-3% rule per operation.
- On the other hand, we choose to go further and invest 10% per transaction.

In this way, we will compare any losses that may be incurred.

We hope that even the most skeptical of the 2-3% rule, after seeing this table, are convinced of how important it is to follow this money management rule. The table goes up to 19 losses in a row - a very unlikely scenario you will say.

But you can see the important difference between the two ways of tradingeven if you only suffer 3 consecutive losses: a scenario that is certainly more possible than the previous one. If we follow the 2-3% rule, we end up with more than $ 18,800, so we have not even lost 10% of our capital.

If, on the other hand, we invest more like 10% per trade, we will end up with less than $ 15,000, meaning we would have burned well over 25% of our initial capital. And the main problems always arise when it comes to recovering lost money: this is why money management strategies all aim to avoid, or at least limit, these situations.

Minimum capital required to start trading cryptocurrencies

Another fundamental point of money management where practically all new traders bang their heads concerns the minimum capital to do online trading. The only rule that new make a mistake in this part is truly mind-boggling. Let's see the different mistakes in detail.

- The first traders who fail are those who start thinking they can get rich within a month, underestimating the complexity of online trading;

- Then there are the traders who know they cannot get rich immediately, but think it is possible in 3 months or a little more, and they only dedicate a few weeks to practice and study;
- Finally, there are those that despite having a long-term money management plan, such as a full year, set too high monthly percentages-

It's time to face reality. In fact, even setting a 10% monthly profit for a full year is really an ambitious goal for traders who are just starting to operate. We are not saying it is impossible, but certainly difficult.

traders seem to follow is the following: invest as much as the minimum deposit required by the broker is.

And there is no bigger mistake a trader can make. Let's take an example. If a broker has a minimum deposit of only $200, and we decide to invest that amount, what earnings could we expect? Well, following the 2-3% rule, we are going to invest from $4 to $6 per trade.

What are the problems that could arise in this situation? Our experience tells us there are basically two issues with this approach.

- **Too low an amount to invest**. Trading platforms usually have a minimum amount to invest for each operation, and they do not necessarily accept "small change" as in this case. For instance, on Binance you cannot buy certain cryptocurrencies if you don't have a certain amount of capital.

- **Greed and boredom.** Emotions are one of the main problems of online trading. Using small amounts of money like this will test a trader's patience.

The result that these two problems can lead to is the same: not respecting the previous 2-3% rule and increasing your exposure on each operation.

In the first case, in fact, perhaps it will not even be possible to invest so little through the trading platform. What if the minimum investment to be made was $10, or $20 or, even worse, $50? In this case, a pillar rule of money management goes to hell.

Other traders, on the other hand, although they may invest so little, may soon stop doing so. The possible gains from these operations would be extremely risky. A trader might say "man, I'm wasting my time earning just a couple of dollars per trade! Today I only made a $5 profit in a whole day!". The next action will be to risk more, which as you know by now is not a very wise idea.

The only golden rule, to always be respected, when it choosing the capital to invest in online trading is the f
Never invest more than you can afford to lose.
If the exchange asks too much for your pocket to ope
you have two choices:

- Wait and set aside this amount, and a li (because often starting with the bare minimu counterproductive as you have seen);
- Look for another exchange.

But never, ever, you will have to decide to jeopard which, if lost, risks creating serious economic pro those who are willing to do all this we can only tell online trading is not for you, as we will see in paragraph.

Earnings expectations are key in money man
Each money management plan obliges the tra monthly earnings goals. And the ease with which m

Choosing a 5% threshold as a monthly goal for cryptocurrency trading or any other type of trading is certainly more realistic. If you think that your earnings would then be too low, you might consider the idea of reinvesting the monthly earnings in the capital to be used for trading.

How is it possible to manage one's capital correctly?

We can answer this simple question in a schematic way.

- ability to minimize losses;
- ability to maximize profits;
- ability to trade only what we can lose;
- trading based on available capital.

Let's try to better explain what has been said.

Let's start by saying that to minimize losses and maximize profits we must already have an excellent strategy in mind and not go to trade randomly. By this we mean that we need a well-defined trading system, or a real action plan.

Subsequently, during the purchase phase, you must do it according to the previously planned strategy, according to your theory, but with the help of software, charts, indicators, etc., made available by your brokers as well. This is because we would like to emphasize the fact that you cannot just login to Binance, take the first asset that passes under the tip of the mouse and bet a certain amount.

If you want to lose everything immediately, you can proceed in this direction, otherwise rely on our advice!

It seems superfluous to remember it but hypocrites do not believe it, whether you like it or not, losses are part of the game. The most important thing to do in the event of a loss is to minimize it as much as possible and this is only possible when trading with self awareness and rationality. A good trader knows this.

Our goal is therefore to maximize profits and minimize losses. No matter which trading system you use, the equation will always be the same.

probability of loss% > probability of winning%.

Let's now analyze another important element, the money to be allocated to trading. Even if it seems silly, the first thing to do is to put your hand on your heart and ask yourself: how much can I afford to lose, without feeling awful? With this we only want to advise you never to deprive yourself of the money necessary to buy what you and your family need daily, but to only risk what you have saved and that you want to use to try to make a profit. This will correspond to the maximum amount of money you can risk losing.

Another very important concept deserves to be mentioned, useful for limiting losses and to which you must pay the utmost attention. This concept is represented by the drawdown, or the amount of money that can be lost in trading, expressed as a percentage of the capital available.

The strategy you decide to adopt must therefore be such as not to present a drawdown that can affect all your capital. The drawdown can therefore be understood as a consecutive negative series of losing trades.

The last point concerns the management of capital. What you have to do is simply the calculation to understand how much to invest in each single operation. You must have in mind the optimal ratio between owned capital and individual investment.

Many of the luminaries in the field of money management, also speak of a law, known as Gresham's Law or Statistical Ruin Law, which indicates the necessary performance that the trader must hold to recover a certain percentage of loss. The table below demonstrates this law.

Loss	Gain to match the loss (%)

10	11
20	25
30	43
40	67
50	100
60	150
70	233
80	400
90	900
99	9900

If we carefully analyze the table, we can see how the recovery percentage grows exponentially with increasing losses.

This table serves to make you understand how, once the initial capital has been lost, it is really difficult to recover it, or rather almost impossible.

Calculation of Money Management

Now we can move on to see how to correctly calculate money management.

The formula to be used for a correct determination is the following.

$$C / 100 * T = S$$

Let's see what all these letters mean.

C = Capital owned;

T = Risk tolerance;

S = Amount that you can invest on a single transaction

Let's take a simple example to understand it better, moving from letters to numbers.

If you have a capital of \$1,000 you can invest \$20, or 2% of the capital.

traders seem to follow is the following: invest as much as the minimum deposit required by the broker is.

And there is no bigger mistake a trader can make. Let's take an example. If a broker has a minimum deposit of only $200, and we decide to invest that amount, what earnings could we expect? Well, following the 2-3% rule, we are going to invest from $4 to $6 per trade.

What are the problems that could arise in this situation? Our experience tells us there are basically two issues with this approach.

- **Too low an amount to invest**. Trading platforms usually have a minimum amount to invest for each operation, and they do not necessarily accept "small change" as in this case. For instance, on Binance you cannot buy certain cryptocurrencies if you don't have a certain amount of capital.

- **Greed and boredom.** Emotions are one of the main problems of online trading. Using small amounts of money like this will test a trader's patience.

The result that these two problems can lead to is the same: not respecting the previous 2-3% rule and increasing your exposure on each operation.

In the first case, in fact, perhaps it will not even be possible to invest so little through the trading platform. What if the minimum investment to be made was $10, or $20 or, even worse, $50? In this case, a pillar rule of money management goes to hell.

Other traders, on the other hand, although they may invest so little, may soon stop doing so. The possible gains from these operations would be extremely risky. A trader might say "man, I'm wasting my time earning just a couple of dollars per trade! Today I only made a $5 profit in a whole day!". The next action will be to risk more, which as you know by now is not a very wise idea.

The only golden rule, to always be respected, when it comes to choosing the capital to invest in online trading is the following. Never invest more than you can afford to lose.

If the exchange asks too much for your pocket to open a trade, you have two choices:

- Wait and set aside this amount, and a little more (because often starting with the bare minimum can be counterproductive as you have seen);
- Look for another exchange.

But never, ever, you will have to decide to jeopardize money which, if lost, risks creating serious economic problems. To those who are willing to do all this we can only tell them that online trading is not for you, as we will see in the next paragraph.

Earnings expectations are key in money management

Each money management plan obliges the trader to set monthly earnings goals. And the ease with which many traders make a mistake in this part is truly mind-boggling. Let's see the different mistakes in detail.

- The first traders who fail are those who start thinking they can get rich within a month, underestimating the complexity of online trading;

- Then there are the traders who know they cannot get rich immediately, but think it is possible in 3 months or a little more, and they only dedicate a few weeks to practice and study;

- Finally, there are those that despite having a long-term money management plan, such as a full year, set too high monthly percentages-

It's time to face reality. In fact, even setting a 10% monthly profit for a full year is really an ambitious goal for traders who are just starting to operate. We are not saying it is impossible, but certainly difficult.

Choosing a 5% threshold as a monthly goal for cryptocurrency trading or any other type of trading is certainly more realistic. If you think that your earnings would then be too low, you might consider the idea of reinvesting the monthly earnings in the capital to be used for trading.

How is it possible to manage one's capital correctly?

We can answer this simple question in a schematic way.

- ability to minimize losses;
- ability to maximize profits;
- ability to trade only what we can lose;
- trading based on available capital.

Let's try to better explain what has been said.

Let's start by saying that to minimize losses and maximize profits we must already have an excellent strategy in mind and not go to trade randomly. By this we mean that we need a well-defined trading system, or a real action plan.

Subsequently, during the purchase phase, you must do it according to the previously planned strategy, according to your theory, but with the help of software, charts, indicators, etc., made available by your brokers as well. This is because we would like to emphasize the fact that you cannot just login to Binance, take the first asset that passes under the tip of the mouse and bet a certain amount.

If you want to lose everything immediately, you can proceed in this direction, otherwise rely on our advice!

It seems superfluous to remember it but hypocrites do not believe it, whether you like it or not, losses are part of the game. The most important thing to do in the event of a loss is to minimize it as much as possible and this is only possible when trading with self awareness and rationality. A good trader knows this.

Our goal is therefore to maximize profits and minimize losses. No matter which trading system you use, the equation will always be the same.

probability of loss% > probability of winning%.

Let's now analyze another important element, the money to be allocated to trading. Even if it seems silly, the first thing to do is to put your hand on your heart and ask yourself: how much can I afford to lose, without feeling awful? With this we only want to advise you never to deprive yourself of the money necessary to buy what you and your family need daily, but to only risk what you have saved and that you want to use to try to make a profit. This will correspond to the maximum amount of money you can risk losing.

Another very important concept deserves to be mentioned, useful for limiting losses and to which you must pay the utmost attention. This concept is represented by the drawdown, or the amount of money that can be lost in trading, expressed as a percentage of the capital available.

The strategy you decide to adopt must therefore be such as not to present a drawdown that can affect all your capital. The drawdown can therefore be understood as a consecutive negative series of losing trades.

The last point concerns the management of capital. What you have to do is simply the calculation to understand how much to invest in each single operation. You must have in mind the optimal ratio between owned capital and individual investment.

Many of the luminaries in the field of money management, also speak of a law, known as Gresham's Law or Statistical Ruin Law, which indicates the necessary performance that the trader must hold to recover a certain percentage of loss. The table below demonstrates this law.

Loss	Gain to match the loss (%)

10	11
20	25
30	43
40	67
50	100
60	150
70	233
80	400
90	900
99	9900

If we carefully analyze the table, we can see how the recovery percentage grows exponentially with increasing losses.

This table serves to make you understand how, once the initial capital has been lost, it is really difficult to recover it, or rather almost impossible.

Calculation of Money Management

Now we can move on to see how to correctly calculate money management.

The formula to be used for a correct determination is the following.

$$C \,/\, 100 * T = S$$

Let's see what all these letters mean.

C = Capital owned;

T = Risk tolerance;

S = Amount that you can invest on a single transaction

Let's take a simple example to understand it better, moving from letters to numbers.

If you have a capital of $1,000 you can invest $20, or 2% of the capital.

If, on the other hand, you want to risk a little more and get to risk 5%, then you have the possibility of investing even $50 per trade.

Substituting the numbers in the formula C / 100 * T = S we have:

$$\$1,000 / 100 * 2 = \$20$$

Let's make a second example.

Initial capital = $100,000

Position size = 15%

Stop size = 2%

Consequently, based on the formula we obtain the following calculation.

$$[\$100,000 \text{ x } 15\%] * 2\% = \$300$$

As you can see, the total risk does not increase when the capital increases. Furthermore, it does not increase when the capital becomes lower. As you can see, the risk factor is constant and is not subject to the fluctuations of your capital. Therefore, we suggest you decide your risk per trade before beginning your trading activity. Remember that having a plan is the only way to avoid being controlled by your emotions.

We advise you not to risk more than 2-3% of your capital on a single trade.

Bitcoin and Cryptocurrency Trading

Chapter 9 - Basic Trading Concepts to Start Making Money

For beginners, day trading cryptocurrencies turns out to be a very difficult activity to assimilate, but above all very expensive in economic terms. This is a very risky and challenging business - buying and selling a cryptocurrency on the same day means trying to make money from a small price fluctuation that occurs over a 24 hour period. For many years, the tools for practicing day trading have been the exclusive preserve of financial institutions and large investors. Today, thanks to broadband internet connections (and a good dose of courage and nerves), everyone can have access to cryptocurrencies and day trading. If you have no heart problems and are ready to try your hand at day trading, this chapter will provide you with some useful tips to avoid making the most common mistakes, which obviously would be paid very dearly.

Develop a business plan

Day trading cryptocurrencies is not a game, and as such it is necessary to plan a strategy to always have revenues, costs and any losses under control, exactly as it happens for any real company. To do this, you will need to develop a full-blown business plan that includes the above mentioned data.

You will need to use a fast computer and a broadband internet connection. It may be worthwhile to invest in a second computer as well, in case the main one runs into problems while you have open positions.

Most likely you will want to start with courses that teach you to predict the trend of the cryptocurrency price and the market in general, i.e. about what is called "technical analysis". It will also be necessary to attend some courses that show you the day trading strategies to be adopted, and above all the management of assets and risk (both during a market operation and in the planning phase of orders).

A projection of both short and long term minimum earnings

Budget planning which must also include the costs associated with day trading operations.

There are many strategies and philosophies that can be adopted in trading for the purpose of making money quickly in the cryptocurrency market. Choose the one that best suits your needs and always stick to it, without changing it based on what happens during daily operations. We will give you these strategies later on in the book, do not worry.

- Track your business based on actual gains and losses. You can do this by answering the following questions once a week, so you are sure you are not missing something. Are you making money?
- What kind of signal are you looking for to have a good reason to enter the market?
- Are you looking for cryptocurrencies whose price is underestimated?

- Are you looking for cryptocurrencies with high liquidity (i.e. with a large trading volume) in order to be able to profit from small price movements?
- Do you know when it's time to close a position?

Anticipate losses

In day trading, losses are common. Nobody is able to avoid them. So expect to have to accept that you were wrong and then have to suffer a loss. It is simply part of the equation.

Expect to face unexpected events

The cryptocurrency market is a difficult market where you are in close contact with large investors (banks, insurance companies, funds, etc.). This means that you will need to be prepared to see large price fluctuations, sometimes characterized by sharp spikes or sudden collapses that are often inexplicably reabsorbed. Basically be ready for anything that might happen to the price of a cryptocurrency.

As with any other business, you should learn trading with paper trading and then, once ready, start using real money.

Fortunately, in this case, today's technologies give us a great hand. All exchanges provide their clients with "demo" accounts in which the financial risk is reduced to zero since real money is not used. Search online to choose one of the many brokers that offer a free trial service. We recommend Binance and Coinbase as always.

Stick to your trading strategy

In this activity it is very easy to be influenced by emotions and the fear of losing money. It is therefore very easy to find yourself closing a potentially profitable position just because initially the price trend was not what we expected. Remember that you have made tremendous efforts to create a trading strategy that has proven to be profitable on a historical basis. So try to fully rely on your market strategy and leave the emotions out of this part of the process.

Avoid changing your trading strategy just because it "doesn't seem to work anymore". Remember that even the best strategies can generate a consecutive series of losses. Make changes to your way of trading based only on the dynamic market trend (for example to face a day of high volatility) and not simply because you are losing money.

Never stop following financial news

It is very important to read financial news regularly so that you can make an informed guess about possible market trends on a daily basis.

Very often the trading platforms include within them a section dedicated to all the most important news relating to the various cryptocurrencies.

There are also numerous websites whose purpose is to share financial news related to cryptocurrencies. For example coinmarketcap.com, cointelegraph.com and investing.com.

Once you close a position, always perform an analysis of all your trades. At the end of the trading day, re-analyze all the trades performed to determine exactly how you performed in each individual trade. Why has a certain operation proved to be profitable? Did you materialize a loss because you didn't properly follow your initial strategy?

Keep a diary of your trading

The diary is a great tool to track all your trades and keep a history of your gains and losses. Fortunately, even in this case, modern technology comes to your aid as Binance and Coinbase include the management of the history of all transactions.

Adapt to market changes

Understand the following concept. You will never know in advance how the cryptocurrency market will move. It is a dynamic entity in continuous and constant evolution. While you should never change your trading strategy simply because you are losing money, it is very important to adapt it to noticeable changes in the market.

Remember to change your strategy only based on changes in the market trend and not based on your emotional state or fear of losing money.

If market volatility increases, it is a smart thing to adapt your strategy to the new scenario. Conversely, making a change to the way you invest your money simply because you have experienced an unexpected loss is by no means a good reason to change your trading philosophy.

Remember that "hope" is not a valid trading strategy. For example, you opened a position based on a certain analysis, but it turned out to be wrong because the market is moving in the opposite direction. In this case you could keep the position open in the hope that the price will rise or fall allowing you to recover the loss. This is not a profitable trading strategy. Instead, you should apply your strategy and scientifically and objectively assess whether there are the conditions for maintaining the market position or whether it is better to close it and suffer the loss.

Stop loss, limit orders and price chasing

Use the "stop loss" for all orders. The "stop loss" is a type of order that automatically closes a position when the amount of money lost reaches a certain limit. This is a way to limit losses when a trade proves wrong.

Use limit orders. In this way your position will be opened only if the price of the cryptocurrency in question reaches a certain limit that you set. It is always better to use this type of order because the price of a cryptocurrency can have a large variation in a few minutes.

Avoid trying to "chase" the price of a cryptocurrency . Let's say you've spotted a cryptocurrency that you think will make you a lot of money, so you proceed to place your limit order. Shortly thereafter, you realize that your order has not been filled because the cryptocurrency price has risen. As a result, you raise the price of the order so that it is executed. This behavior is commonly referred to as "chasing" the price and should normally be avoided. Remember that your goal is to buy a cryptocurrency at the correct price and not buy it at any cost simply to have your order executed.

If you study and follow these principles you will be on your way to be more profitable than 99% of every cryptocurrency trader. Please, read this chapter again at least a couple of times to make sure these concepts enter in your subconscious mind.

Chapter 10 - Paper Trading

In the previous chapter we have mentioned paper trading. In the following pages we dive a bit deeper into this topic, as it's an interesting learning tool you have at your disposal when you are just starting out.

Many people today are attracted to online trading. Of these people, however, more than half are blocked in proceeding with trads by the fear that their inexperience could lead to a huge loss of money. Cryptocurrency trading is not an easy operation, but neither is it a step in the dark. And this above all thanks to the possibility of taking the first steps in financial operations through simulation. For those who, for example, want to start trading cryptocurrency, we recommend a fairly effective simulation technique to learn online trading: Paper trading.

Paper trading is, to all intents and purposes, a trading forecast, without the use of real cash. In the financial sector, Paper trading has a long history. In fact, in the past, Paper trading was carried out precisely on sheets of paper.

Then progress gave us a set of faster tools. Today, having a PC (but also a tablet or a smartphone), it is possible to do Paper trading through specific platforms or with an Excel table. When doing paper trading, you should take note of the following data.

- Opening price and closing price;
- Number of exchanges;
- Type of operation;
- Profits and Losses;
- Total costs;
- Percentages of gain or loss.

Let's talk about Paper trading associated with cryptocurrency. In fact, in this case the operations can be so fast and unpredictable that most likely there would not even be time to transcribe some data.

For beginners, the ideal would be to start by registering on an online exchange platform, opening a demo account. Through a demo account it will be possible to start trading cryptocurrency, in a fictitious way, to become familiar with online trading. Even with a simple demo account you can start collecting useful data to carry out a Paper trading.

Both the tracking of the trades and the creation of the graphics could, at first glance, seem remarkably complicated. To overcome this inconvenience and to allow the use of online paper trading to all interested parties, many broker platforms offer numerous training courses, with e-books and video tutorials, to effectively learn all the notions of online trading. A great broker you can use to do cryptocurrency paper trading is Etoro. Binance and Coinbase have a very limited interface and possibility when it comes to paper trading. However, they will be the go to place for when you will feel ready to put real money on the line.

Another plus of Paper trading regards money management. In fact, as we have seen in a previous chapter, to become successful traders, it is not only important to know how to make correct forecasts, but also to learn how to manage your capital to make the most of these forecasts.

To get good, you need a lot of experience. In fact, we recommend using a demo account for at least six months, before starting to trade with real money. The simulation period will also be important to study cryptocurrency trading in greater detail. It is essential to know the markets and the types of financial transactions there are, refine strategies and learn forecasting techniques. Finally, you will also need to learn and implement the best way to manage your capital, as described in chapter 8.

Conclusion

Congratulations on making it to the end of this book, we hope you found some useful insights to take your cryptocurrency trading skills to the next level. As you should know by now, the world of cryptocurrency is extremely complicated and there is a new "opportunity" every way you look. However, our experience tells us that only by taking things seriously and having a proper plan you can develop your trading skills to the point that you can trade for a living.

Our final advice is to stay away from the shining objects that the world of cryptocurrencies offers you every day. Choose a cryptocurrency you want to master and study it in depth. After you have a sufficient knowledge on what you are talking about, apply the fundamental and technical analysis strategies we have discussed in this book. Analyze your results, improve your money management skills and become the master of your emotions.

As you can see, there are no shortcuts you can take. Easy money does not exist. What exists is the possibility to start from zero and work your way up to become a professional trader. The journey might be difficult, but it is certainly worth it.

To your success!

Charles Swing and *Masaru Nakamoto*

Bitcoin and Blockchain

Master the Technology behind the Number One Cryptocurrency and Learn how to Buy, Hold and This New Asset Class – Discover how to Earn Passive Income on Your Bitcoin!

misuse of the information in question by the reader will render any resulting actions solely under their purview. There are no scenarios in which the publisher or the original author of this work can be in any fashion deemed liable for any hardship or damages that may befall them after undertaking information described herein.

Additionally, the information in the following pages is intended only for informational purposes and should thus be thought of as universal. As befitting its nature, it is presented without assurance regarding its prolonged validity or interim quality. Trademarks that are mentioned are done without written consent and can in no way be considered an endorsement from the trademark holder.

Table of Contents

Introduction

Bitcoin has taken the world by storm once again when it crossed $20,000 per BTC in December of last year. After more than 2 years of bear market, the most famous cryptocurrency surpassed its previous all time high.

A lot of people are now trying to improvise themselves as professional investors and are losing a lot of money, only helping those who actually know what they are doing accumulate an incredible amount of wealth that will lead to generational fortunes.

To join the club of the few investors that actually make it, you need the right strategies and the right mindset. Notice how we did not include a large initial capital. In fact, while having more money to trade with means having more fire power, it is not necessary to have thousands of dollars to accumulate Bitcoin and build wealth.

In fact, when we started investing in Bitcoin we only had a few hundreds to put into the market, but that sum yielded us thousands and thousands of dollars over the span of a few years.

In this book you are going to discover all the strategies that have allowed us to take investing skills to the next level and everything that helped us understand Bitcoin. If you diligently apply our advice, we are sure you are going to see amazing results in a relative short period of time, since this bull run is offering an amazing number of opportunities.

Please, stay away from all the shiny objects of the cryptocurrency world. Just focus on Bitcoin, study it deeply and then milk it like a cash cow!

To your success!

Charles Swing and *Masaru Nakamoto*

Chapter 1 - Bitcoin Scams and How to Avoid Them

The blockchain industry has several cryptocurrency-related scams. Some of the most common include blackmail, fake exchanges, fake giveaways, social media phishing, copy-paste malware, phishing emails, Ponzi and pyramid schemes, and ransomware. In this chapter we are going to analyze some of these scams, so that you have the knowledge not to fall for them. In fact, when it comes to Bitcoin and cryptocurrency, the most important thing is being able to protect your assets. We are sure the next few pages are going to be extremely important.

Until new technologies are introduced to the world, scammers will continue to search for new tricks to deceive victims. Sadly, Bitcoin gives scammers in the crypto industry an interesting opportunity by being a borderless digital currency.

The decentralized nature of Bitcoin allows you to be in full control of your tokens. However, it also makes it more difficult to design an adequate regulatory and legal framework, as we have seen in a previous chapter. If scammers manage to convince you to make mistakes while using Bitcoin, they could steal your BTC, and there is practically nothing you can do to get back your coins.

That said, it is vital that you understand how scammers operate and find out how to identify potential red flags. There are a ton of scams involving Bitcoin to keep an eye out for. In this chapter we discuss the most common ones.

Blackmail

Blackmail is a method used by many scammers to threaten victims with the disclosure of sensitive information unless rewarded in some way. This reward typically comes in the form of a cryptocurrency payment.

In this scam, criminals obtain sensitive information about the victim and exploit it to force them to send Bitcoin or other forms of money.

The best way to avoid blackmail and protect your bitcoins is to be very careful when selecting your login credentials, which sites you visit online and who you give your information to. Also, using two-factor authentication whenever possible is another great help. If the information you are being blackmailed with is false and you find it out before sending the payment, you may be out of trouble.

Fake exchanges

As the name suggests, fake exchanges are fraudulent copies of legitimate crypto exchanges. Typically, these scams present themselves as mobile apps, but you may also find them in the form of desktop apps or fake websites. Some fake exchanges are very similar to the original versions, so you need to be very careful. They may seem legitimate at first glance, but their goal is to steal your money.

Typically, these fake exchanges attract crypto traders and investors by offering them free cryptocurrencies, competitive prices, minimal fees, and even gifts. To avoid getting scammed on a fake exchange, you should save the real URL as a bookmark in your browser and always double check before logging in. You can also use Binance Verify, a tool that allows you to verify the legitimacy of URLs, Telegram groups, Twitter accounts, and more.

For mobile apps, check out the developer's information, number of downloads, reviews and comments.

Fake giveaways

Fake giveaways are used to steal cryptocurrencies by offering something for free in exchange for a small deposit. Typically, scammers will ask you to first send funds to a Bitcoin address in order to receive more bitcoins in return (e.g., "send 0.1 BTC to receive 0.5 BTC"). However, if you make these transactions, you will not receive anything and you will never see your funds again.

There are many variations of scams involving fake giveaways. Instead of BTC, some scams will ask for other cryptocurrencies, such as ETH, BNB, XRP and many others. In some cases, they may ask for your private keys or other sensitive information.

Fake giveaways are usually found on Twitter and other social media platforms, where scammers latch onto popular tweets, viral news, or announcements (like a protocol update or an upcoming ICO).

The best way to avoid this type of scam is to never participate in any kind of giveaway that requires you to submit something of value first. Legitimate giveaways will never ask for funds.

Social media phishing

Social media phishing is a common Bitcoin scam that, like fake giveaways, it is often found on social media platforms. First of all, the scammers create an account that resembles that of someone with a high level of authority in the crypto industry. After that, they will offer fake giveaways via tweets or direct messages.

The best way to protect yourself from social media phishing is to verify that the person is really who they say they are. Some platforms have indicators to find out, such as checking verified accounts on Twitter and Facebook.

Copy-paste malware

Copy-paste malware is a very stealthy method used by scammers to steal your funds. This type of malware tampers with data on your device and, if you are not careful, it tricks you into sending money directly to the scammers.

Let's say you want to send a payment in BTC to your friend Bob. As usual, he sends you his Bitcoin address so you can copy and paste it into your wallet. However, if your device is infected with copy-paste malware, the scammer's address will automatically replace Bob's address the moment you paste it. This means that as soon as your Bitcoin transaction is sent and confirmed, you will have paid the scammer and Bob will not receive the coins.

To avoid this type of scam, you need to pay close attention to the security of your computer. Be wary of suspicious messages or emails that contain infected attachments or dangerous links. Pay attention to the websites you visit and the software you install on your devices. You should also consider using an antivirus and periodic scans for threats. Also, it's important to keep your device's operating system up-to-date and manually check the address before confirming the transaction.

Phishing emails

There are different types of phishing. One of the most common involves phishing emails that try to trick you into downloading an infected file or clicking a link that leads to an apparently legitimate malicious website. These emails are especially dangerous when they simulate a product or service you use frequently.

Typically, scammers include a message urging you to take urgent action to protect your account or funds. They may ask you to update your account information, reset your password or submit documents. In most cases, their goal is to get your login credentials and try to hack your account.

The first step in protecting yourself from phishing is to check if the emails are from the original source. If in doubt, you can contact the company directly to confirm that the email received was sent by them. Additionally, you can move your mouse over the email links (without clicking) to check if the URLs have misspellings, unusual characters, or other irregularities.

Even if you don't find any warning signs, you should avoid clicking on these links. If you need to log into your account, do it in another way, such as manually typing the URL or using your saved bookmarks.

Ponzi and pyramid schemes

Ponzi and pyramid schemes are two of the oldest financial scams. A Ponzi scheme is an investment strategy that distributes returns to long-time engaged investors using the funds added by new investors. When the scammer can no longer introduce new investors, the money stops flowing. OneCoin is a good example of a Ponzi scheme in crypto.

A pyramid scheme is a business model that pays members based on the number of new members they introduce. When the new members run out, the money runs out.

The best way to avoid these scams is to research cryptocurrencies before buying them - be it an altcoin or Bitcoin. If the value of a cryptocurrency or a Bitcoin fund is solely dependent on the enrollment of new investors or members, it is likely a Ponzi or pyramid scheme.

Ransomware

Ransomware is a type of malware that blocks victims' mobile devices or computers or prevents them from accessing important data - unless a ransom is paid (usually in BTC). These attacks can be particularly destructive when they target hospitals, airports and government agencies.

Typically, the ransomware will block access to important files or databases and threaten to delete them if payment is not made within the deadline. Unfortunately, however, there are no guarantees that the criminals will honor their promise.

There are some measures that allow you to protect yourself from ransomware attacks. The best practices are the following.

- Install an antivirus and keep your operating system and applications up to date.
- Do not click on suspicious advertisements and links.
- Pay attention to email attachments. You should be especially wary of .exe, .vbs or .scr files).
- Backup your files regularly to restore them in case of an attack.

As you might have noticed, the world of Bitcoin could be extremely dangerous if you do not put in place the right protective measures. However, if you are careful and have the right knowledge, it is also the most secure method to store your wealth. Please, dedicate some time to the study of this topic, as it as important as deciding your investing strategy.

Chapter 2 - Bitcoin Update: the Lightning Network

In this chapter we are going to discuss a very interesting topic, that forever changed the history of the Bitcoin network when it was implemented. We are talking about the Lightning Network. Let's take a closer look at what it is.

The Lightning Network concept was created by Joseph Poon and Thaddeus Dryja in 2015. The main idea behind the project is the development of a payment protocol that can be used as an off-chain solution to address the problem of the scalability that plagues the Bitcoin blockchain, although the concept is also applicable to other cryptocurrencies.

The introduction of the Lightning Network is the answer to the limitations that both Bitcoin and many other cryptocurrencies face. Currently, the Bitcoin blockchain is capable of processing 2 to 7 transactions per second. With the growth of the cryptocurrency ecosystem and with more and more people joining the network, transactions transmitted to the blockchain are likely to increase. Gradually, the network becomes more and more congested and the overall performance is compromised, significantly reducing the practical usability of Bitcoin as a global digital currency. In this context, the Lightning Network was created as an attempt to reduce the congestion of the Bitcoin blockchain network.

How the Lightning Network works

The Lightning Network is composed of an off-chain transfer network developed on the Bitcoin blockchain. The system operates at a peer-to-peer (P2P) level and its use is based on the creation of so-called "two-way payment channels", through which users can perform direct cryptocurrency transactions.

When two counterparties decide to open a payment channel, they have the ability to transfer funds from one wallet to another. Even though the process of creating a new payment channel involves an on-chain transaction, all transactions that take place within the channel are off-chain and do not require global consent. As a result, these transactions can be quickly executed through a smart contract, incurring significantly lower fees and a significantly higher TPS (transactions per second) rate.

To open a payment channel, the two interested counterparties must set up a multi-signature wallet and add funds to it. The funds within the multi-signature wallet are accessible only when the private keys of both parties are provided (two or more, depending on the case). This means that one of the parties cannot access the wallet without the consent of the other.

As an example, suppose Alice wants to use the Lightning Network to trade bitcoins with Bob. First of all, the two open a payment channel, using a multi-signature wallet. While the payment channel works like a smart contract, the multi-signature wallet acts as a safe, where the funds to be exchanged are deposited. As long as the payment channel remains open, Alice and Bob can perform as many off-chain transactions as they want.

Immediately after each transaction, both Alice and Bob sign and update their copy of the balance sheet, which records the number of coins in their possession. When they no longer need it, they can close the payment channel and transmit the final balance to the Bitcoin blockchain. The Lightning Network smart contract guarantees that both parties will receive their bitcoins, based on the final version of the financial statements.

In other words, participants only need to interact with the Bitcoin blockchain twice. One to open the payment channel and one to close it. As a result, all transactions performed within the channel do not interact directly with the main chain.

Network Routing

Even if two counterparties do not have a direct payment channel available, they can still send and receive bitcoins through interconnected payment channels. This means that Alice can send funds to Charlie without having to create a direct channel with him, as long as there is a route between them that contains sufficient funds.

Therefore, if Alice has an open payment channel with Bob and Bob has a channel with Charlie, Alice can send bitcoins through Bob. Payment routing may involve several nodes of the Lightning Network, but the smart contract will automatically search for the shortest path available.

Benefits of the Lightning Network

As we have seen, the Lightning Network project is working to achieve an off-chain solution that solves the scalability problem. If successful, it could reduce traffic on the Bitcoin blockchain. Through the use of two-way payment channels, the Lightning Network makes almost instant transactions possible.

The Lightning Network could prove suitable for micropayments, as it allows the transfer of very small amounts, even reaching 1 satoshi. In addition, the machine-to-machine economy could implement automated micropayments, in which transactions are performed between electronic devices without the need for human intervention.

Limits of the Lightning Network

Unlike on-chain transactions, within the Lightning Network it is not possible to make payments if the recipient is offline. Therefore, the network participants may need to monitor payment channels regularly to protect their funds (this risk can be eliminated by using external monitoring services).

Furthermore, the Lightning Networkis not suitable for large payments. The network is based on several multi-signature wallets (in practice shared wallets), and it is very likely that these do not contain a sufficient balance to act as intermediaries for large payments. Opening and closing a payment channel requires an on-chain transaction, which usually requires labor and higher fees.

When will the Lightning Network be implemented?

Taking into consideration the beta version of the mainnet announced by Lightning Labs, the launch date of the Lightning Network had been set for March 15th, 2018. However, the Lightning Network has not yet been actually implemented on the Bitcoin blockchain.

Following the launch of the beta, there has been a huge increase in the number of Lightning Network nodes and payment channels. Some exchanges, like Kraken, announced that they will start supporting the Lightning Network in 2021.

The collective work of nodes and payment channels is what makes Lightning Network an interesting solution to the problem of scalability. The beta version is currently being tested and its efficiency is yet to be proven. Despite this, the Lightning Network has enormous potential to improve the Bitcoin and cryptocurrency ecosystem.

The Lightning Torch

On January 19, 2019, pseudonymous Twitter user "hodlonaut" began a game-like promotional test of the Lightning Network by sending 100,000 satoshis (0.001 bitcoin) to a trusted recipient where each recipient added 10,000 satoshis to send to the next trusted recipient. The so-called "lightning torch" payment reached notable personalities. Among them there were Lightning Labs CEO Elizabeth Stark, Twitter CEO Jack Dorsey, and Binance CEO "CZ" Changpeng Zhao. The lightning torch was passed 292 times before reaching the formerly hard-coded limit of 4,390,000 satoshis. The final payment of the lightning torch was sent on April 13th, 2019 as a donation of 4,290,000 satoshis ($217.78 at the time) to Bitcoin Venezuela, a non-profit association that promotes bitcoin in Venezuela. We had the privilege to participate in the Lightning Torch and we are extremely proud of that event.

Chapter 3 - The SegWit Update

Segregated Witness (SegWit) is an update to the protocol developed in 2015. The concept was introduced as a solution to the scalability problem that blockchain networks still face today.

On average, the Bitcoin network validates a new block every 10 minutes, each containing several transactions. Consequently, the size of the block affects the number of transactions that can be confirmed in each block. Currently, the Bitcoin blockchain is capable of processing around 7 transactions per second.

The core idea of SegWit is to reorganize the block data so that the signatures are no longer placed along with the transaction data. In other words, the SegWit update consists of separating witnesses (signatures) from transaction data. This allows multiple transactions to be stored in a single block, thus increasing the performance in terms of transactions on the network.

Considering that Bitcoin can process around 7 transactions per second, executing a transaction can sometimes take a long time. This process is far slower than conventional payment solutions and financial networks, which can process thousands of transactions per second.

SegWit was developed in 2015 by Bitcoin developer Pieter Wuille, along with other Bitcoin Core contributors. In August 2017, the SegWit update was implemented as a soft fork on the Bitcoin network.

There are several cryptocurrency projects using SegWit today, including Bitcoin and Litecoin. The protocol update brought with it a number of benefits, including improved transaction speed and increased block capacity. Additionally, SegWit has fixed the so-called transaction malleability bug (more on that later).

Increase in block capacity

One of the biggest advantages of SegWit is the increase in block capacity. By removing signature data from transaction input, more transactions can be stored in a single block.

Transactions are made up of two main components: inputs and outputs. Essentially, an input contains the public address of the sender, while the output contains the public address of the recipient. However, the sender must prove ownership of the funds they are transferring, and they do so with a digital signature.

Without SegWit, signature data can take up to 65% of a block. With SegWit, the signature data is removed from the transaction input. This brings the actual block size from 1MB to approximately 4MB.

It is important to note that SegWit is not an actual block size increase. Instead, it is an advanced solution that allows you to increase the actual size without having to increase the block size limit (which would require a hard fork). To be more precise, the current block size is still 1MB, but the actual block size limit is 4MB.

SegWit also introduced the idea of block weight. We can consider the weight of the block as a concept that replaces the idea of block size. Essentially, the block weight is a measure that includes all data in the block, including transaction data (1MB) and signature data (3MB), which are no longer part of the input field.

Increased transaction speed

By creating a block that can hold more transactions, SegWit has also made it possible to increase transaction speed, as there can be a larger number of transactions moving through the blockchain. While a block may take the same time to mine, more transactions are being processed in it, so the transactions per second rate is higher.

The increase in transaction speed has also helped reduce transaction costs in the Bitcoin network. Before SegWit, it wasn't uncommon to spend more than $30 on a transaction.

However, SegWit has drastically lowered this cost to less than $ 1 per transaction.

Correction of transaction malleability

In the past, a major problem with Bitcoin was the ability to potentially alter transaction signatures. If a signature is altered, it could result in the corruption of a transaction between two parties. Since the data stored on blockchains is virtually immutable, it would have been possible to permanently store invalid transactions on the blockchain.

With SegWit, signatures are no longer part of the transaction data, which removes the possibility of altering this data. This fix has enabled further innovations in the blockchain community, including second-layer protocols and smart contracts.

SegWit and Lightning Network

The development of second-layer protocols was partially made possible by the correction of the transaction malleability bug. In a nutshell, second-layer protocols are new platforms or new products developed on top of a blockchain, such as that of Bitcoin. As we have seen in the last chapter, one of the best known second-layer protocols is Lightning Network, an off-chain micropayment network.

SegWit vs SegWit2x

SegWit is a soft fork upgrade, which means it is backwards compatible. In other words, Bitcoin nodes that are not updated to include SegWit are still capable of processing transactions. However, another SegWit implementation called SegWit2x (S2X) has been proposed, which would have required a hard fork upgrade.

The key difference between SegWit and SegWit2x is that the latter would not only involve a change in transaction batching, but also an increase in block size (from 1MB to 2MB). However, a larger block size would have increased the load on node operators and miners, as it would have led to double the amount of data to manage.

Another important difference is that the SegWit proposal was supported and enforced by the Bitcoin community. The episode gave birth to the concept of UASF, which stands for user-activated soft fork.

Conversely, SegWit2x proposed a substantial change to one of Bitcoin's core rules, and as the developers did not reach a consensus on its adoption and implementation, the SegWit2x movement was suspended.

SegWit's implementation marked the biggest update to the Bitcoin protocol, and the fact that it has been supported and implemented by the decentralized community makes it even more important.

The introduction of SegWit was a major step forward in solving many problems related to Bitcoin and other blockchain networks - especially in terms of scalability. Through the combination of SegWit and second-layer protocols, blockchain networks can handle more transactions, with more efficiency and lower costs.

Despite being a powerful and innovative solution, SegWit has not yet reached full adoption. Currently, the percentage of Bitcoin addresses using SegWit is around 53%.

Chapter 4 - Schnorr Signatures

As you may know, Bitcoin enforces property rights through what we call the Elliptic Curve Digital Signature Algorithm (or ECDSA). The algorithm allows you to take a number (i.e., a private key) and derive a public key from it.

The magic of this step is that while it is simple for you to get the public key from the private key, the reverse is impossible. Your private key is your passport to the Bitcoin network. It is what allows you to generate an address to receive coins and spend them later.

In this chapter, we will talk about the Schnorr signature algorithm, an alternative to ECDSA that could introduce some interesting changes in Bitcoin.

A summary on digital signatures

Digital signatures work just like their ancestors on pen and paper, but they are much more secure. With a little time and effort, anyone can forge a signature on paper. You can't do the same with a solid digital signature scheme, even with hundreds of thousands of years at your disposal.

There are several use cases for digital signatures. One of the most popular involves proving to the world that you wrote a particular message. As mentioned, you can create a public key from a private key. To do this, just perform some mathematical fantasy on the secp256k1 curve. After that, you can also generate a public address from your public key. Wait, you don't know what the secp256k1 curve is? Do not worry, if you are just starting out studying Bitcoin, it is not something worth explaining as it has more to do with cryptography than cryptocurrencies.

You just need to know that it is completely safe to show your public key to anyone. You can add it to your website or Twitter bio to allow others to verify your identity. Likewise, you can share your public addresses with others to transfer cryptocurrencies.

Your private key allows you to create a digital signature. By writing a message and performing an operation on it using your private key, you create a signed message. Anyone can review it and compare it to your public key to verify that it was indeed signed by you.

How does this relate to Bitcoin? Whenever you make a transaction in Bitcoin, you are digitally signing a message that says "I am sending these coins which have previously been sent to me". Then, when it is sent to the other nodes on the network, they can check that the ECDSA signature matches the message. If not, the nodes reject it.

What are Schnorr's signatures?

Schnorr signatures are a different type of algorithm. It operates similar to the Elliptic Curve Digital Signature Algorithm we currently use, but has a number of advantages over it. Schnorr's signatures are actually older than the ECDSA, which leads many to wonder why they haven't been integrated into Bitcoin from the start.

One possible explanation is that Claus P. Schnorr - the creator of the algorithm - patented them. The patents expired in early 2008, months before the publication of the Bitcoin whitepaper, but the algorithm still lacked general standardization. For this reason, Satoshi Nakamoto has opted for the more widely accepted (and open source) ECDSA.

Benefits of Schnorr signatures

Schnorr's signatures are quite simple in comparison to other algorithms. As a result, they are safer than their alternatives. It might not mean much at first glance, but they have another powerful feature: linearity.

Simply put, this makes the algorithm particularly attractive for certain businesses - in particular, for multi-signature transactions. You may know that Bitcoin already supports multi sigs, but not in the best way.

When you create a multisignature address, anyone who sends you funds does not need to know what conditions you have set for spending inputs. They may not even know they are sending funds to a multisig setup. In fact, the only noticeable difference of the address is the fact that it starts with a "3".

However, you reveal its nature when you want to move funds. Let's assume you used a 2-of-3 setup with Alice and Bob. To spend 5 BTC, all three of you must provide public keys and valid signatures. When you move the funds out of the address, the entire network can know what happened by examining the blockchain.

From a privacy standpoint, that's not good news. Also, if you create a larger multisig (e.g., 8-of-10), you are taking up a lot of space on the blockchain. This can be expensive, as it will result in a longer transaction - remember that the more bytes there are in your transaction, the more you will have to pay to get it through the network.

Schnorr's signatures were presented as a solution to these privacy and scalability issues. They allow things like signature aggregation, which combines the signatures of several signers into a single signature. The resulting "master signature" will be

Chapter 5 - Taproot

A long with Schnorr's signatures, Taproot is a highly anticipated Bitcoin tech upgrade since the introduction of SegWit. Taproot's goal is to change the way Bitcoin scripts operate to improve privacy, scalability and security. This and much more will be possible by combining Taproot with a related update, Schnorr's signatures. Anyone familiar with the crypto community knows that privacy, scalability and security are top priorities. Even though Bitcoin is the most popular cryptocurrency in the world, those issues still need to be addressed. Taproot aims to do exactly that.

Bitcoin has had its ups and downs, but it has proven to be the pillar holding the crypto universe in place. Regardless of incidents over the years, such as the hack against Mt.Gox or the famous Bitcoin hard forks, the crypto community has continued to support Bitcoin.

However, there are certain issues that cannot be ignored and one of the biggest is privacy. Bitcoin is a public blockchain, anyone can monitor the transactions that take place on the network. For some people, this is a major problem.

You can increase your anonymity through techniques such as coin mixing and CoinJoins. Unfortunately, none of these make Bitcoin a private currency. While the same goes for Taproot, it could help increase anonymity on the network. The Taproot update is considered by many to be an important first step in resolving Bitcoin's lack of privacy and other related issues. But what exactly is Taproot, and how will it benefit Bitcoin? Let's find it out together.

What is Taproot?

Taproot is a soft fork that improves Bitcoin scripts to increase privacy and other factors related to complex transactions. Transactions on the Bitcoin network can use various features that make them more complex, including timed issues, multi-signature requirements, and more.

Without Taproot, anyone can identify transactions that use these complex features, which require the creation of multiple transactions. However, the Taproot update will allow you to "hide" all the moving parts of a Bitcoin transaction that includes such complexities. Therefore, even if the transactions adopt these functions, they will appear as a single transaction. This is a big win for Bitcoin privacy advocates.

In fact, Taproot allows you to completely hide the execution of a Bitcoin script. For example, spending Bitcoin using Taproot can make a transaction in a Lightning Network channel, a peer-to-peer transaction, or a sophisticated smart contract indistinguishable. However, it should be noted that this does not change the fact that the wallets of the initial sender and the final recipient will be exposed.

The Taproot proposal was initially presented by Greg Maxwell, developer of Bitcoin Core, in January 2018. In October 2020, Taproot was integrated into the Bitcoin Core library after a pull request from Pieter Wuille. To fully implement the update, node operators must adopt Taproot's new consensus rules.

Depending on this dynamic, the actual implementation could take months.

The benefits of Taproot for Bitcoin

As we have already mentioned, Taproot will bring major improvements to Bitcoin's privacy. Combined with Schnorr's signatures, Taproot could also increase the efficiency in executing transactions. In addition to increased privacy, other potential benefits include the following.

> Reduced amount of data to be transferred and stored in the blockchain;
> More transactions per block (higher transactions per second rate);
> Reduced transaction costs.

Another advantage of Taproot is the fact that signatures will no longer be malleable, a known security risk in the Bitcoin network. Simply put, the malleability of signatures means that it is technically possible to change the signature of a transaction before it is confirmed. By doing so, the attack would make it appear that the transaction never took place. This leaves Bitcoin vulnerable to the notorious double spend problem, which could ruin the integrity of the distributed ledger.

As you may understand by now, Taproot is a highly anticipated and widely supported upgrade to Bitcoin. When implemented alongside Schnorr's signatures, we will see dramatic improvements in privacy, scalability, and security. Additionally, these updates can generate increased interest in the Lightning Network and encourage multi-signature solutions as the industry standard.

Regardless of the level of your involvement in the Bitcoin community, the benefits of improving privacy, efficiency and security will likely affect your experience when using Bitcoin. We could not be more excited for this incredible update!

Chapter 6 - Bitcoin and the Evolution of the Web

The internet has changed dramatically since its creation. From Internet Relay Chat (IRC) to modern social media, it has become a vital part of human interactions - and continues to evolve.

Web 3.0 is the next generation of Internet technology, and it relies heavily on the use of machine learning and artificial intelligence (AI). Its goal is to create more open, connected and smarter websites and web applications that focus on automated data understanding.

Through the use of AI and advanced machine learning techniques, Web 3.0 aims to deliver more personalized and relevant information at a faster rate. This is possible thanks to the use of intelligent search algorithms and developments in Big Data analytics.

Current websites typically have static information or user-posted content, such as forums and social media. While this allows information to be distributed to a large group of people, it may not meet the needs of a specific user. A website should be able to personalize the information it offers to each individual user, similar to the dynamics that characterizes human communication in the real world.

In Web 3.0, an ocean of information will be available to websites and web applications, which will be able to understand and use data in a way that is relevant to the individual user.

A brief history of the evolution of the Internet

Websites and web applications have changed dramatically over the past few decades. They have evolved from static sites to data-driven sites that users can interact with and modify.

Web 1.0

The original internet was based on what is now known as Web 1.0. The term was coined in 1999 by the author and web designer Darci DiNucci, to distinguish between Web 1.0 and Web 2.0. In the early 1990s, websites were being developed using static HTML pages that could only display information - there was no way for users to modify the data.

Web 2.0

That all changed in the late 1990s as the transition to a more interactive Internet began to take shape. With Web 2.0, users could interact with websites through the use of databases, server-side processing, forms and social media.

This has led to the transition from a static web to a more dynamic one. Web 2.0 has brought with it a greater emphasis on user-generated content and interoperability between different sites and applications. Web 2.0 was less observation and more participation. By the mid-2000s, most websites had made the transition to Web 2.0.

The future of the internet

Looking at the history of the Internet, the evolution of a more semantically intelligent web is logical. The data was initially presented statically to users. Later, users could interact with this data dynamically. Now all this data will be used by algorithms to improve the user experience and make the web more personalized and familiar.

Web 3.0, even if not yet fully defined, could exploit peer-to-peer (P2P) technologies such as blockchain, open-source software, virtual reality, Internet of Things (IoT) and much more. Currently, many applications are limited to running on a single operating system. Web 3.0 could enable applications by making them more device-agnostic, meaning they could operate on different types of hardware and software without any additional development costs.

Web 3.0 also aims to make the Internet more open and decentralized. In today's environment, users have to rely on network and telephony service providers to monitor the information passing through their systems. With the introduction of distributed ledger technologies, this could change very soon, and users could get their data back in their hands.

The advantages of Web 3.0

Web 3.0 offers huge advantages over its predecessors. Some of the benefits are the following.

- **No central points of control.** As middlemen are removed from the equation, user data is no longer under their control. This reduces the risk of censorship by governments or corporations and reduces the effectiveness of denial-of-service (DoS) attacks.

- **Greater interconnectivity of information**. As more products connect to the Internet, larger data sets give the algorithms more information to analyze. This can help them ensure more accurate information that meets the specific needs of the individual user.

- **More efficient navigation.** In the past, finding the best search engine result was quite challenging. However, over the years, these have improved in finding semantically relevant results based on the search context and metadata. This results in a more convenient web browsing experience that can help anyone find the exact information they need with relative ease.
Web 2.0 has also introduced social tagging systems, which can be manipulated. With smarter algorithms, manipulated results can be filtered by AI.

- **Improved advertising and marketing**. Nobody likes to be bombarded with online advertisements. However, if the ads are relevant to the user's interests and needs, they can be useful instead of just being a waste of time. Web 3.0 aims to improve advertising by leveraging smarter AI systems and distinguishing specific audiences based on consumer data.

- **Best customer support**. When it comes to websites and web applications, customer service is key to a positive user experience. However, due to the enormous costs many successful web services fail to expand their customer service operations in a timely manner. Through the use of smarter chatbots that can speak to multiple customers at the same time, users can enjoy a superior experience when dealing with support agents.

The evolution of the internet has been a long journey and will certainly continue on to further iterations. With the enormous increase in data available, websites and web applications have the ability to move to a web that offers a significantly better experience to a growing number of users around the world.

While there is no concrete definition for Web 3.0 yet, it is already in place thanks to innovations in other technological fields and Bitcoin is certainly playing a role in this revolution, creating a smarter finance for everyone.

Chapter 7 - Improving the

Blockchain Scalability

In previous chapters we have mentioned the different updates that are being implemented on the Bitcoin blockchain to make it more scalable. In the next few pages we are going to dive deeper into this topic.

With the term scalability we refer to the skill of a system to grow to satisfy an increasing request. In computer technology, you could improve your device's performance by updating the hardware to make it faster in performing certain activities. When we talk about scalability in Blockchain, we refer to the growth of their ability to manage more transactions.

Protocols like Bitcoin have many strengths, but scalability is not one of these. If Bitcoin is managed in a centralized database, it would be relatively easy for an administrator to increase speed and performance. However, the value proposals of Bitcoin (e.g., resistance to censorship) require that many participants synchronize a copy of Blockchain.

Blockchain scalability problems

Performing a Bitcoin node is relatively cheap, and even simple devices can do it. Despite this, given that thousands of nodes must keep up to date with each other, there are some limits on their ability.

Limits are fixed on the number of transactions that can be processed on-chain, to prevent the database from being too heavy. If it became too big too quickly, the nodes could not keep up. Also, if the blocks are too large, it is not possible to send them quickly through the network.

As a result, we are faced with an obstacle. A blockchain can be seen as a train service that departs at defined intervals. Each wagon offers limited places, and to get a ticket. Travelers must make an offer to earn the place. If everyone tries to get on the train at the same time, the price will be high. Similarly, a clogged network with pending transactions will require users to pay higher commissions to ensure that their transactions are included in reasonable times.

A solution could be to enlarge the wagons. This would like to say more places, higher performance and lower prices for tickets. But there are no guarantees that places are not filled as in the previous case. The wagons cannot be enlarged constantly, as well as blocks on blocks and gases cannot expand to infinity. The latter makes it more expensive for nodes to stay on the network, as they need more advanced hardware to stay synchronized.

The creator of Ethereum, the second largest cryptocurrency, Vitalik Buterin coined the scalability trilemma to describe the challenge that blockchains must face. Butterin has theorized that protocols must compromise between scalability, safety and decentralization. These elements are in conflict between them. In fact, by concentrating too much on two of the properties, you will neglect the third one.

For this reason, many see scalability as something to reach off-chain, while security and decentralization should be maximized on the blockchain itself.

Off-chain scalability solutions

Off-chain scalability refers to approaches to perform transactions without weighing off the blockchain. Protocols that connect to the blockchain and allow users to send and receive funds, without transactions to appear on the main chain.

What is a sidechain?

A sidechain is a separate blockchain that is not an independent platform, as it is anchored in some way to the main chain. The main chain and the sidechain are interoperable, and the assets can flow freely from one to the other.

There are several ways to ensure that the funds can be transferred. In some cases, assets are moved from the main chain by depositing them into a special address. In fact, they are not actually sent to the sidechain - they are instead blocked in the address, and a corresponding amount is issued on the sidechain. A more linear option is to send funds to a custody service, which exchanges the deposit in funds on the sidechain. However, in this case centralization could become an issue.

The functionality of a sidechain

Suppose your friend Alice has five bitcoins. She wants to exchange them for five equivalent units on a Bitcoin sidechain - let's call it sidecoin. The sidechain in question uses a bidirectional anchorage, so users can transfer their own assets from the Main Chain to the Sidechain and vice versa.

Remember that the Sidechain is a separate blockchain. Therefore, it will have blocks, nodes and mechanisms of different validation. To receive the sidecoin, Alice sends the five bitcoins to another address. It could be owned by someone who will credit the five sidecoin on her address once you received bitcoins. Alternatively, you could present some kind of trust-minimized configuration where the sidecoin are automatically credited when the software detects a payment.

Alice has now converted her coins into sidecoin, but she can always reverse the process to recover her bitcoins. Now that she has entered the sidechain, she is free to make transactions on this separate blockchain. She can send sidecoin or receive from others, just as it would happen on the main chain.

She might, for example, pay Bob a sidecoin for a logo. When she wants to go back to Bitcoin, she could send her four remaining sidecoin to a special address. Once the transaction is confirmed, four bitcoins would be unlocked and sent to an address that you control on the main chain.

Use cases of a sidechain

Maybe you're wondering what all this can serve. Why does not Alice directly use the Bitcoin blockchain?

The answer is that the sidechain could be capable of things that bitcoin is unable to do. Blockchain are accurately organized compromise systems. Although Bitcoin is the safest and most decentralized cryptocurrency, it is not the best in terms of performance. Bitcoin transactions are faster than conventional methods, but still relatively slow compared to other blockchain systems. The blocks are mined every ten minutes, and the commissions can grow greatly when the network is congested.

Indeed, it is likely that this level of security is not necessary for small daily payments. If Alice is paying a coffee, she will not wait for confirmation of the transaction. Her coffee would be cold before the payment is concluded.

The sidechain are not bound by the same rules. In fact, they don't even need to use the proof of work to operate. You can use any consensus mechanism, trust a single validator, or change any parameter. You can introduce updates that do not exist on the main chain, produce larger blocks and impose quick regulations.

It is interesting to note that the sidechain could have critical bugs and it would not influence the underlying chain. This allows them to be used as a platform for experimentation and to implement functionality that would otherwise require consent from the majority of the network.

Provided that users are satisfied with compromises, sidechains could be a fundamental step towards effective scalability. The main chain nodes must not file every transaction from the sidechain. Alice could enter the sidechain with a single Bitcoin transaction, run hundreds of sidecoin transactions, and exit the sidechain. As for the Bitcoin Blockchain, she performed only two transactions - one to enter and one to go out.

Payment channels

Payment channels have the same purpose as the Sidechain on the scalability front, but are fundamentally very different. Like the sidechain, they push the transactions out of the main chain to prevent the blockchain from clogging. Unlike sidechain, however, they do not require a separate blockchain to work.

A payment channel uses a Smart Contract to allow users to perform transactions without publishing them on the blockchain. This is possible thanks to the use of an agreement imposed by software between the two participants.

How does a payment channel work?

In models like the famous Lightning Network, two parts first deposit the coins in an address they possess together. This is a multi-signature address, which requires two signatures to spend the funds. So, if Alice and Bob have created this address, the funds can only be moved with the consent of both.

Suppose they deposit 10 BTC each at an address that now contains 20 BTCs. It would be easy for them to keep a budget that begins by saying that Alice and Bob have 10 BTC each. If Alice wants to give Bob a coin, they could update the budget indicating that Alice has 9 BTC and Bob has 11 BTC. They should not publish the results on the Blockchain until they continue to update these budgets.

When they decide to end their transactions, they could create a transaction that sends these balances to the addresses in possession of the parts, sign it and transmit it.

Alice and Bob may have registered ten, one hundred or a thousand transactions on their budget. But as far as the blockchain is concerned, only two on-chain operations performed: one for the initial transaction and the other to realize the funds at the end. In addition to these two, all other transactions are free and almost instant. There are no costs to pay for miners and no confirmation of the block to wait.

Obviously, the example we discussed above requires the collaboration of both parties, a situation not ideal for two strangers. However, you can use special mechanisms to punish any fraud attempt, so that the parties can certainly interact without trusting each other.

Payment routing

Evidently the payment channels are convenient for two parts that provide a high volume of transactions. But it does not end here. It is possible to create a network of these channels to ensure that Alice can pay a participant to which it is not directly connected. If Bob has an open channel with Carol, Alice can pay her, as long as there is sufficient capacity. Alice will transmit the funds to the side of the Bob channel, which, in turn, will transmit them to that of Carol. If Carol is connected to another participant, she can do the same thing.

A network of this type evolves in a distributed typology in which anyone is connected to different peers. We will often find multiple paths to a destination, and users can choose the most effective one.

We discussed two scalability approaches that allow transactions to be carried out without weighing off the underlying blockchain. Both technologies, sidechain and payment channels, must still mature, but are already widely exploited by users who want to circumvent the deficiencies of transactions in the base level.

Over time and as other users join the network, it is important that decentralization remains intact. This is only possible through the imposition of limits on the growth of the blockchain to ensure that new nodes can easily join.

Supporters of off-chain scalability solutions believe that, over time, the main chain will only be used to regulate high-value transactions, or to enter/exit Sidechain and open/close channels.

Chapter 8 - The Stock to Flow Model

In this chapter we are going to take a look at a price prediction model called stock to flow. In simple terms, the Stock to Flow model (SF or S2F) is a way to measure the abundance of a particular resource. The Stock to Flow ratio is the quantity of resources present in the reserves divided by the quantity that is produced annually.

The Stock to Flow model is generally applied to natural resources. Let's take the example of gold. Although estimates may vary, the World Gold Council estimates that around 190,000 tons of gold have been mined in history. This quantity (that is, the total supply) is what we can call the stock. In addition, approximately 2,500 to 3,200 tons of gold are mined each year. This quantity is what we call the flow.

We can calculate the Stock to Flow ratio using these two parameters.

But what does it mean in real life terms? Essentially it shows how many new units of a given resource enter the market each year, in relation to the total supply. The higher the Stock to Flow ratio, the less new supply enters the market relative to the total. Therefore, an asset with a high Stock to Flow ratio should, in theory, hold its value effectively over the long term.

Conversely, consumer goods and industrial products will generally have a low Stock to Flow ratio. For what reason? Since their value typically comes from their destruction or consumption, the stocks are usually only sufficient to cover the demand. These assets don't necessarily have a high value as possessions, so they tend to perform poorly as an investment asset. In some exceptional cases, the price could rise rapidly if a shortage is foreseen in the future. But other than that, production remains in step with demand.

It is important to emphasize that scarcity alone does not necessarily mean that a resource is precious. Gold, for example, is not that rare - after all, we have 190,000 tons available! The Stock to Flow report suggests that it is valuable because the annual production compared to the existing supply is relatively small and constant.

The Stock to Flow ratio of gold

Historically, gold has had the highest Stock to Flow ratio of all precious metals. But what is the exact number? Going back to our previous example - divide the total supply of 190,000 tons by 3,200, and you will get a Stock to Flow ratio of ~ 59. This tells us that, at the current rate of production, it would take around 59 years to mine 190,000 tons of gold.

However, it is worth bearing in mind that the estimates of the amount of new gold that will be mined each year are just that - estimates. If we increase the annual production (flow) to 3,500, the Stock to Flow ratio drops to ~ 54.

While we're at it, why not calculate the total value of all the gold that has been mined in history? If we take a price of around $ 1500 for every ounce of gold, the total value of all gold reaches around $9 trillion. That said it sounds like a lot, but if we combined all this gold into a cube we could make it fit on a single soccer field!

For comparison, the highest total value of the Bitcoin network hit $1 trillion at the beginning of 2021.

Stock to Flow and Bitcoin

By now you should know how Bitcoin works. Therefore, it won't be hard for you to understand why it might make sense to apply the Stock to Flow model to it. Essentially, this model treats bitcoins as limited resources, like gold or silver.

Gold and silver are often referred to as resources that act as a store of value. In theory, they should hold their long-term value due to their relative scarcity and low flow. Furthermore, it is somewhat difficult to significantly increase the supply in a short period of time.

According to supporters of the Stock to Flow model, Bitcoin is a similar asset. It is scarce, relatively expensive to produce, and its maximum supply is limited to 21 million coins. Furthermore, the issuance of supply of Bitcoin is defined at the protocol level, which makes the flow completely predictable. You should have already familiarized with the concept of halving, where the amount of new supply entering the system is halved every 210,000 blocks (roughly four years).

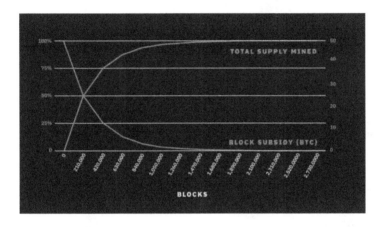

According to the proponents of this model, the combination of these properties creates a scarce digital asset with deeply valid characteristics for maintaining long-term value. Furthermore, they assume that there is a statistically significant relationship between the Stock to Flow and the market value. According to the model's projections, Bitcoin's price is expected to go through a noticeable increase over time due to its consistently low Stock to Flow ratio.

Among others, the application of the Stock to Flow model to Bitcoin is often attributed to PlanB and its article "Modeling Bitcoin's Value with Scarcity".

Bitcoin's Stock to Flow ratio

The current circulating supply of Bitcoin is around 18 million bitcoins, while the new supply is around 0.7 million per year. At the time of writing, Bitcoin's Stock to Flow ratio is hovering around 50.

In the image below, you can see the historical relationship between the 365-day moving average of Bitcoin's Stock to Flow and its price. We have also indicated the dates of the Bitcoin halving on the vertical axis.

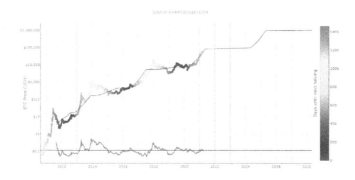

Limits of the Stock to Flow model

While Stock to Flow is an interesting model for measuring scarcity, it doesn't explain all parts of the picture. The models depend entirely on their assumptions. First of all, Stock to Flow is based on the assumption that scarcity, as measured by the model, should bring value. According to critics of the Stock to Flow, this model fails if Bitcoin has no other useful quality besides supply shortages.

Gold's scarcity, predictable flow and global liquidity have made it a relatively stable store of value relative to fiat currencies, which are subject to devaluation. According to this model,

Bitcoin's volatility is also expected to decrease over time. This is confirmed by historical data provided by Coinmetrics.

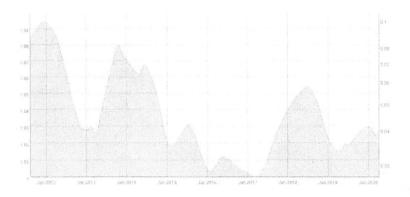

The valuation of an asset requires consideration of its volatility. If volatility is to some extent predictable, the valuation model may be more reliable. However, Bitcoin is famous for its large price swings.

While volatility may decrease at the macro level, Bitcoin has been valued in a free market since its inception. This means that the price is mostly self-adjusted on the free market by users, traders and speculators. Combining this with relatively low liquidity, Bitcoin is likely to be exposed to sudden spikes in volatility more than any other asset. Hence, the model may fail to consider this either.

Other external factors, such as economic Black Swan events, could undermine this model. However, it should be noted that this possibility essentially applies to any model that tries to predict the price of an asset based on historical data. A Black Swan event, by definition, has a surprise factor. Historical data cannot take into account unknown events.

Our opinion is that the Stock to Flow model has been incredibly accurate so far and that it will be able to predict future price movements for the foreseeable future.

Chapter 9 - Revolutionizing the Banking System

B anks often act from intermediaries within the global economy by managing and coordinating the financial system through their internal registers. Given that these registers are not available to the public to be examined, people are forced to pay confidence in the banks and in their infrastructures often obsolete.

Blockchain technology has the potential to revolutionize not only the world's money market, but also the entire banking industry, eliminating these intermediaries and replacing them with a trustless, borderless, transparent and easy to access for everyone.

Blockchain could potentially help make the transactions fastest and most economical, increase access to capital, ensure greater data security, make trustless agreements through Smart Contract, make compliance easier and much more.

Moreover, thanks to the innovative nature of the blockchain, the ways in which new financial items can interact with each other can potentially lead to completely new types of financial services.

Advantages of the blockchain for the banking system

The blockchain offers different advantages that can truly help the banking system become more trustless and decentralized. Here are the main benefits the blockchain can provide to our financial system.

- **Security**. Blockchain-based architecture eliminates individual error points and reduces the need to deliver data into the hands of intermediaries.

- **Transparency**. The blockchain standardizes shared processes and creates a single shared source of truth for all network participants.

- **Trust**. Transparent registers allow different parts to collaborate and make agreements easier.
- **Programmability**. The blockchain allows reliable automation of commercial processes through the creation and execution of smart contracts.

- **Privacy**. Privacy Technologies made possible from BlockChain allow selective sharing of data between companies.

- **Performance**. Networks are designed to support a large number of transactions, at the same time supporting interoperability between different chains, thus creating an interconnected blockchain network.

Rapid transfer of funds using the blockchain

Sending money into the current banking system can be a rather long process, can impose various commissions for banks and customers and can request additional checks and administration. In the instant connectivity era, the traditional banking system failed to keep up with the rest of technological developments.

Blockchain technology offers a faster payment method and with lower commissions, available at any time, without borders and with the same security guarantees that the traditional system can offer.

Asset tokenization on the blockchain

Buying and selling titles and other assets, such as actions, bonds, commodity, currencies and derivatives, requires a complex and coordinated effort between banks, brokers, compensation agencies and exchange platforms. This process should not only be efficient, but accurate as well. The added complexity directly corresponds to the increase in times and costs.

Blockchain technology simplifies this process by providing a basic technological level that makes tokenization of any type of asset possible. Given that much of the financial assets is bought and sold digitally through online brokers, the tokenization on the blockchain seems to be a convenient solution for all interested parties.

Some innovative blockchain companies are looking for physical asset tokenization, such as real estate, works of art and raw materials. This would make the transfer of the asset property with a convenient and economical process in the real world. Furthermore, it would offer new opportunities for investors with a limited capital, allowing them to buy a fractional property of expensive assets - investment products that could not be accessed before.

Loan grant using the blockchain

Banks and other loan companies have monopolized the credit sector, thus managing to offer loans with relatively high interest rates and limit access to capital based on credit scores. This makes the process of concession of long and expensive loans. While banks have the advantage, the economy depends on the supply by the banks of the funds necessary for high-cost products, such as cars and houses.

Blockchain technology allows anyone in the world to participate in a new type of loan ecosystem, which is part of the movement often defined as decentralized finance (DEFI). To create a more accessible financial system, the DEFI aims to develop and offer all financial applications on the blockchain. Peer-to-peer money loans, allowed by the blockChain, allow everyone to lend and borrow in a simple, safe and inexpensive way, without arbitrary restrictions. With a more competitive loan sector, banks will be forced to offer better terms to their customers.

The impact of the blockchain on global trade

Participation in international trade is extremely evident due to a large number of international standards and regulations imposed on importers and exporters. Keeping track of goods and moving them through each phase still requires manual processes, full of documentation and handwritten records.

Blockchain technology allows participants from commercial finance to provide a higher level of transparency thanks to a shared register that accurately monitors moving goods in the globe. Simplifying and optimizing the complex world of commercial finance, blockchain technology allows importers, exporters and other companies to save large amounts of time and money.

Safe agreements via smart contract

Contracts exist to protect people and businesses when they enter into agreements, but this protection has a high cost. Due to the complex nature of contracts, the process necessary to create one requires a lot of manual work by legal experts.

Smart contracts allow the automation of the agreements through deterministic code testing tampering running on the BlockChain. Money can remain safe at ESCROW and is released only when certain conditions of the agreement have been met.

Smart contracts substantially reduce the element of trust necessary to reach an agreement, minimizing the risks linked to financial agreements and the chances of ending up in court.

Integrity and security of data enabled by the blockchain

The sharing of data with trusted imminators always involves the risk that the data is compromised. Furthermore, many financial institutions still use paper-based storage methods, which significantly increases accounting costs.

BlockChain technology enables optimized processes that automate verification and data recording, digitize KYC / AML data and transaction history, and makes real-time authentication of financial documents possible. This helps reduce operational risks, the risk of fraud, and reduces costs related to data management for financial institutions.

The banking and financial sector is one of the main sectors that will be revolutionized by the blockchain. The potential cases of use are numerous, from real-time transactions to asset tokenization, loans, simpler international trade, safer digital agreements and much more.

The resolution of all the technological and regulatory difficulties that hinder the potential of this new financial infrastructure seems to be just a matter of time. A bank and financial system based on a trustless, transparent and borderless base level is the most effective tool for creating a more open and interconnected economy.

Chapter 10 - Bitcoin Blockchain and Safety

In this book we have often mentioned that the blockchain is an incredible safe and secure technology to store transactions. But what makes it so secure? Well, in this chapter we are going to dive deeper into this aspect.

Blockchain are protected through a variety of mechanisms, including advanced cryptographic techniques and behavioral and decision-making mathematical models. Blockchain technology is the structure below most of the cryptocurrency systems and is what prevents duplication or destruction of this type of digital money.

The use of blockchain technology is currently under development in other contexts in which immutability and data security are very valuable. Some examples include the registration and monitoring of beneficial donations, medical databases, and management of logistics chains.

However, blockchain security is certainly not a simple topic. Therefore, it is important to understand the concepts and basic mechanisms that give solid protection to these innovative systems.

The concepts of immutability and consensus

Although there are many elements that contribute to the security associated with blockchain, two of the most important are the concepts of consensus and immutability. The consensus refers to the capacity of the nodes within a distributed network blockchain to agree on the actual state of the network and on the validity of the transactions. Generally, the process to achieve consensus depends on the so-called consent algorithms.

Immutability, on the other hand, refers to the ability of the blockchain to prevent alteration of those transactions that have already been confirmed. Although these transactions are often linked to the transfer of cryptocurrencies, they can also refer to the registry of other forms of digital data.

Combined, consensus and immutability provide data security structure in the blockchain network. While the consensus algorithms guarantee that the rules of the system are followed and that all the parties involved agree on the current state of the network - immutability guarantees the integrity of data and transaction records after each new data block is confirmed as valid.

The role of encryption in the safety of Blockchain

Blockchains make extensive use of encryption to get their data security. A cryptographic function that takes on extreme importance in this context is hashing. Hashing is a process in which a known algorithm as a hash function receives a data input (of any size) and returns a determined output that contains a fixed length value.

Regardless of the dimensions of the input, the output always has the same length. If the input is changed, the output will be completely different. However, if the input does not change, the resulting hash will always be the same - no matter how many times the hash function is performed.

Inside blockchain, these output values, known as hashes, are used as unique identifiers for data blocks. The hash of each block is generated in relation to the previous block hash, a factor that connects the blocks together, thus forming a chain. Furthermore, the block hash depends on the data contained within it, so any changes to the data would also require the modification of the block hash.

As a result, each block hash is generated based on both the data contained within it and on the previous block hash. These hash identifiers play a fundamental role in ensuring the safety and immutability of the blockchain.

Hashing is also exploited in the consent algorithms used to validate transactions. In the Bitcoin Blockchain, for example, the Proof of Work (POW) algorithm used to reach consensus and for mining new units exploits a hash function called SHA-256. As the name suggests, SHA-256 transforms the input data into a 256-bit long hash or 64 characters.

In addition to providing protection for transactions stored on the registers, encryption is also used to guarantee the safety of the wallets used to store the tokens. The pair of public and private keys that allow users to receive and send payments is created through the use of asymmetrical or public key cryptography. Private keys are used to generate digital signatures for transactions, allowing you to authenticate the property of transferring tnits.

It is not necessary to go down to the details for the purpose of this chapter, it is enough to know that the nature of asymmetrical encryption prevents anyone except for the owner of the private key to access the funds preserved in a cryptocurrency wallet, thus maintaining such funds safe until when the owner decides to spend them (as long as the private key is not shared or compromised).

Crypto Economy

In addition to encryption, a relatively new concept known as crypt economics plays a role in maintaining the security of the blockchain network. It refers to the study field known as game theory, which mathematically formulates decision-making processes of rational actors in situations with predefined rules and rewards. While the traditional game theory can be applied to a wide range of cases, the crypto economy model specifically describes the behavior of nodes within distributed blockchain systems.

In short, the crypto economy is the study of the economic aspect of blockchain protocols and the possible results that their design could submit according to the behavior of the participants. Security through crypto economy is based on the notion that blockchain systems offer better incentives to nodes that honestly act instead of adopting malicious or incorrect behavior. Again, the proof of work consensus algorithm used in the mining of Bitcoin offers an excellent example of this incentive scheme.

When Satoshi Nakamoto created the structure for Bitcoin mining, the process was intentionally conceived as expensive in terms of resources. Due to its complexity and its computational needs, the mining process involves a considerable investment of time and money - regardless of where the mining node is located. As a result, this structure places a strong disincentive to malicious actions and remarkable incentives for honest mining activities. The dishonest or inefficient nodes are quickly expelled from the blockchain network, while honest and efficient miners have the potential to receive substantial rewards for blocks.

Similarly, this balance of risks and rewards also guarantees protection from potential attacks that aim to compromise consent by accumulating the majority of the Hash Rate of a blockchain network in the hands of a single group or entity. These attacks, known as 51 percent attack, could be extremely harmful if performed successfully. Due to the competitiveness of the mining proof of work and the size of the Bitcoin network, the probability that an attacker is able to get control of the majority of nodes is really minimal.

Furthermore, the cost of the computational power necessary to obtain 51 percent of the control of a huge blockchain network would be astronomical, placing an immediate disincentive to such a huge investment for a potential small reward. As long as the cost linked to establishing a majority of dishonest nodes remains prohibitive and there are better incentives for honest activity, the system will be able to thrive without significant disorders. It should be emphasized that smaller blockchain networks are undoubtedly susceptible to the attacks described above, given that the total hash rate dedicated to these systems is considerably lower than that of bitcoin.

Through the combined use of game theory and encryption, blockchains are able to reach high levels of security as distributed systems. However, as for almost all systems, it is essential that these two fields of knowledge are adequately applied. An accurate balance between decentralization and safety is vital for the development of a reliable and effective network.

As the cases of use of blockchain continue to evolve, even security systems will develop to meet the needs of various applications. Private blockchain currently under development for commercial enterprises, for example, make greater reliance on safety through access control instead of based on the mechanisms of game theory that are essential for the security of many public blockchains.

Chapter 11 - The 2021 Bull Market

M arket trends are among the most fundamental aspects of the financial markets. We can define a market trend as the general direction in which an asset or market moves. For this reason, market trends are closely monitored by technical analysts and fundamental analysts.

Bull markets tend to be relatively easy to exploit, as they allow for the use of the simplest trading and investment strategies. Even inexperienced investors could perform well in really favorable bull market conditions. However, it remains crucial to understand that markets move in cycles.

So what should you know about bull markets? How do investors take advantage of bull markets? You can find the answers in this chapter.

What is a bull market?

A bull market (or bull run) is the scenario in a financial market where prices are rising. The term bull market is often used in the context of the stock market. However, it can be used in any financial market - including Forex, bonds, commodities, real estate, and cryptocurrencies. Furthermore, the expression bull market could also refer to a specific asset such as Bitcoin or Ethereum. It could describe a sector, such as utility tokens, privacy coins, or biotech stocks.

You may have already heard Wall Street traders use the terms "bullish" and "bearish". When an investor says he is bullish in a market, it means that he expects prices to rise. When bearish, he predicts a drop in prices.

Often being bullish can mean having a long position in the market, but this is not necessarily the case. A bullish condition may not present a long opportunity at the moment but simply indicates that prices are rising or are expected to rise.

It is also important to highlight the fact that a bull market does not mean that prices do not fall or fluctuate. For this reason it is more reasonable to consider bull markets over longer time frames. In this sense, bull markets will include periods of decline or consolidation without invalidating the overall market trend. Take a look at the Bitcoin chart below. Despite periods of decline, and some violent market crashes, it has been in an overall bullish trend since its inception.

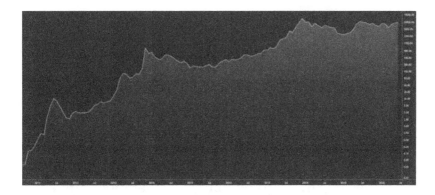

In this perspective, the definition of a bull market depends on the time periods that are taken into consideration. Generally, when we use the term bull market we are talking about a time span of months or years. As with other techniques used in market analysis, trends observed over longer periods tend to have more value than trends over shorter periods.

Thus, in a bull market over extended periods there may be prolonged phases of decline. These countertrend price movements are known for their particular volatility - although this can vary a lot from asset to asset.

Examples of a bull market

Some of the best-known examples of bull markets come from the stock market. We are talking about scenarios in which the prices of stocks and market indexes (such as the Nasdaq 100) are constantly increasing.

Taking the global economy into consideration, we know it fluctuates between bull and bear markets. These market cycles can last for years or even decades. Some argue that the bull market that began following the 2008 financial crisis and ended due to the coronavirus pandemic was the "longest bull market in history." The validity of this claim is uncertain - as we said, bull markets over longer periods of time can be a matter of point of view.

Anyway, let's take a look at the long-term performance of the Dow Jones Industrial Average (DJIA). We can see that it is basically in a century-long bull market. Of course, there are periods of decline that can last for years, as in the case of 1929 or 2008, but the overall trend is still heading upwards.

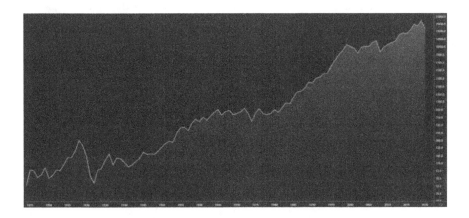

Some argue that we could see a similar trend in Bitcoin, but we can't say for sure when Bitcoin will face a multi-year bear market. Importantly, most other cryptocurrencies will likely never experience such appreciation, so be very careful what you invest in.

Bull market vs. bear market

These are opposite concepts, so the difference isn't very hard to guess. In a bull market, prices continually rise, while in a bear market, prices continually fall.

This also results in differences on the best methods for investing in the two conditions. In a bull market, investors will generally want to be long, while in a bear market they will want to be short or out of the market sitting on cash.

In some cases, even sitting on cash (or stablecoins) can mean being short on the market, as this means expecting prices to drop. The main difference is that holding the funds in cash is more about preserving capital, while a short position is meant to gain on falling asset prices. However, if you sell an asset with the intention of buying it back at a lower price, you are essentially in a short position - even if you are not directly profiting from the decline.

Another element to consider are fees. Staying in stablecoin is unlikely to lead to fees, as there are usually no costs associated with custody. Conversely, many short positions will require a financing fee or interest rate to ensure they are opened. As such, quarterly futures may be ideal for long-term short positions, as they do not charge funding fees.

How investors can benefit from bull markets

The central idea in bull market investing is relatively simple. Prices are going up, so opening long and buying corrections is generally a reasonable strategy. For this reason the buy and hold strategy and dollar cost averaging plan are generally suitable for long-term bull markets.

There is a saying that goes: "The trend is your friend, until it isn't anymore." This simply means that it makes sense to trade in the direction of the market trend. At the same time, no trend will last forever, and the same strategy may not perform well in other parts of a market cycle. The only certainty is the fact that markets can and will change. As we have seen for the COVID-19 pandemic, multi-year bull markets can be wiped out in a matter of weeks.

Of course, most investors will be bullish in a bull market. It makes sense as prices are rising, so overall sentiment should be bullish as well. However, even during a bull market, some investors will be bearish. If their investing strategy allows it, they may also be successful with short-term bearish trades.

Hence, some investors will try to open short on recent highs in a bull market. However, we are talking about advanced strategies that are generally more suited to professional investors. For less experienced investors, it usually makes more sense to trade following the market trend. Many investors get trapped when they try to make money shorting bull markets. After all, facing a raging bull can be a dangerous.

Chapter 12 - Earning Passive Income on Bitcoin

We would like to end this book with a chapter dedicated to how you can use the bitcoins you bought to earn passive income. This is a great strategy if combined with the dollar cost averaging technique we have explained in a previous chapter. Before explaining to you how you can do this, it is important to know that it involves a third party company, called Blockfi. If you have read the entire book you know how much it is important to have full control of your private keys when you own cryptocurrencies. Blockfi is the only crypto related company we trust, as they have proven to be transparent and give regular proof of ownership of the funds. They have an affiliate program as well, but we will not share with you our affiliate link, because we do not want you to think we have an interest in recommending you this company.

Now that we have cleared this out, let's dive deeper into what Blockfi is and why it is an amazing company to earn interest on your bitcoins.

Blockfi is a cryptographic asset management platform that offers its users the opportunity to earn interests on their tokens. It offers loans in cryptocurrencies, StableCoin and USD to companies and organizations that try to monetize their resources.

This is perhaps the easiest way to make your cryptocurrencies generate passive income on the Blockfi platform. Once an account is opened you can deposit and start earning compound interests from day one.

You can create an Interest blockfish account by visiting the Blockfi website and to do so you must be at least eighteen. You have to go through a KYC process, where you have to upload a clear photo of your identity card. If all the details are correct, your account is approved in a few minutes. If your account has not been approved within 48 hours, you can write to onboarding@blockfi.com to get assistance and complete the verification process. For business accounts, you will need to send the identification information of managers and owners of your company's shares. Blockfi also offers promotions to attract customers and currently offers a registration bonus up to $250 with a deposit of at least $25 or higher. As we said you are asked to complete your KYC precisely because this helps the Blockfield Organization to prevent money laundering activities and other similar illicit practices.

The Blockfi interest account provides interests on deposits on the first working day of each month. A minimum balance is not required to earn interests. If you don't have some of the coins supported by the platform, you can transfer USD or EUR directly into your Blockfi interest account. Traditional FIAT money will be converted into any of the coins available. Rates may vary taking into account different factors, but they will provide you with information in advance about this. Furthermore, interest rates change once every two or three months compared to other platforms that change the rates on a weekly basis. Therefore, Blockfi provides rather constant earnings over time.

Blockfi also offers some flexibility in payments. If you are depositing your funds in a particular form of cryptocurrency, you can earn interest in the cryptocurrency of your choice. For example, if you have deposited BTC, you can earn in the form of BTC, ETH, LTC, USDC or USDT. You need to change this information at least two working days before the last working day of the month, so that the choice is respected with the right timing. Otherwise, if you don't, you will earn interest on the type of cryptocurrency you have originally deposited.

Blockfi also provides monthly statements that indicate the funds you give, the interest you have earned and the interests you can earn next month. Blockfi will send you monthly statements by email and you can also download them in PDF format directly from the platform. You can also download the transaction history in CSV file format in the appropriate section of your personal account. Furthermore, you can also filter transactions in a specific date range and download the report.

Blockfi generates interest by providing its funds to trusted companies and institutional borrowers, purchasing ETFs and other financial securities. An in-depth credit analysis is performed before lending money to anyone. You can also close your account whenever you prefer. If your portfolio has cryptocurrencies, you can transfer them to other accounts along with the related accrued interests. If you do not deposit any amount within sixty days from the opening of your account, it will be automatically closed by the system.

Cryptographic loans

The minimum loan amount is $10,000 and you can deposit Bitcoin, Ethereum or Litecoin as collateral. Money is then transferred to the customer account in dollars. Blockfi promotes this service as an ideal way to finance purchases of considerable entities, such as properties, cars, holidays and the like, or as an opportunity to diversify your financial portfolio.

How to use the blockfi trading platform

Blockfi users can also deposit funds on the platform and use them to buy more cryptocurrencies or stableCoin.

Blockfi has its own Exchange, which is available to all its users with a personal account. This allows investors on the platform to switch from one cryptocurrency to another in an intuitive way.

The best part is that you still earn compound interests while you trade.

To register for a Blockfi account, follow these simple steps:

- Visit the Blockfi website and create an account;
- Complete the email verification and access your account;
- Add funds to the account via the user's dashboard;
- Click "Exchange" in the Navigation Panel located at the top;

- Select the cryptocurrency you want to exchange;
- Enter the amount you want to buy;
- Review the order details and click Enter to finalize the transaction.

Blockfi introduced a new feature that allows users to send cash deposits by bank transfer to the platform. This involves Fiat currency transmission to buy stablecoins directly on the platform. The process is rather easy for beginners who have never bought Bitcoin before. They can register with Blockfi, deposit traditional currencies by bank transfer and receive up to 8.6% in a Blockfi interest account. USD dollar deposits are automatically exchanged in Gemini Dollars (GUS) which can then be converted into Bitcoin, Ethereum, Litecoin and USDC using the Blockfi trading platform.

To buy stablecoins using USD with Blockfi, follow these steps:

- Access your BlockFlen account.
- Click "Deposit" in the top navigation bar
- Select "USD (bank transfer)" as a deposit currency.

- Select "Bank transfer" as a payment method
- Enter your details and send your bank transfer to Blockfi

The Blockfi team

The company was founded in 2017 and is based in New Jersey. Its co-founders are Zac Prince and Flori Marquez, who serve respectively as CEO and SVP of operations. Prince has a degree in International Business at Texas State University and a technology background, having been vice-president of business development at Orchard Platform and sales manager at Sociomantic Labs. Marquez, graduated from Cornell and is one of the rising stars in the banking and financial sector. Rene Van Kesteren is Chief Risk Officer and spent thirteen years at Bank of America Merrill Lynch before joining Blockfi. The other main member of the executive group is the CTO Mahesh Paolini-Subramanya, who worked in the technological sector since he graduated from the University of Notre Dame at the end of the 1980s.

The rest of the managerial team has a similar mix of experience in Fintech and traditional finance, while the company as a whole employs 65 people distributed in four offices between New Jersey, New York, Argentina and Poland.

One of the most reliable metrics when evaluating a relatively new company is its list of initial investors. Blockfi has impressive support in this field, including Akuna Capital caliber actors, coellid ventures, Galaxy Digital Ventures and the Winklevoss twins.

How Blockfish works

If you are trying to earn interest, get a loan or trading, you can only do it with Bitcoin, Ethereum or Litecoin.

When it comes to loans, you need more capital to be deposited as a guarantee to benefit from the minimum loan of $10,000. The maximum loan to value ratio (LTV) is 50%, with additional rates available.

It is worth discussing exactly how these loans are structured.

The requests are processed rapidly and, if you apply in a working day, you can wait for a decision from Blockfi in about two hours. Blockfi uses several factors to calculate interest rates, including the amount of the loan, location and particular warranty provided. This is undoubtedly of great attraction for those in the cryptocurrency space that are trying to get rid of some restrictions that traditional finance puts in place. Obviously, if the value of the collateral has increased in that time frame, you may be able to recover some of the expenses commissions. Conversely, if the collateral value suddenly decreases, you may need to provide additional funds or pay the loan balance.

Who can use blockfi?

The company identified "three main types of organizations" that use the services provided:

- **Traders and investment funds.** Essentially those looking for arbitrage opportunities that need to borrow cryptocurrencies to close the price spreads between different markets. "Margin" traders may also have to contract loans to cover the costs of their trading strategies

- **"Over the Counter" market operators (OTC).** These are buyers and sellers wishing to do business away from public exchanges, which often have high commissions.

- **Companies that need liquidity in cryptocurrencies.** They may want to maintain most of their resources in Cold Wallets but they still need liquidity to provide ordinary operations of their customers. The Crypto ATMs can be quoted as an example.

Blockfi commissions

Users who create a Blockfi interest account will then be subject to limits and withdrawal commissions as follows:

- Bitcoin: commission of 0.0025 BTC and 100 per week limit
- Ethereum: commission of 0.0015 ETH and $5K limit per week
- Litecoin: commission of 0.0025 LTC and limit of $10,000 per week
- Stablecoins: commission of $0.25 USD and $1 million limit per week

There is no minimum balance to earn interests with blockfi.

You can also enjoy a free withdrawal of cryptocurrencies and stablecoins every month and you can collect it at any time you prefer. Each free withdrawal applies for a single cryptocurrency every month. After making a request, your cryptocurrency will first be transferred to Blockfi Trading LLC and later at the requested address. If you want to make an additional withdrawal, you will be charged the relevant commission as we have listed before.

Blockfi and safety

The main custody Exchange of Blockfi is Gemini, (of the famous Winklevoss brothers) which has recently completed a "SoC 2" compliance conformity, which made it the first exchange of cryptocurrencies to achieve this level of security. The exchange is regulated by the Department of Financial Services of the New York State (NYDFS) and retains 95% of its resources in a Cold Wallet. According to the website, in fact, even the same twins would not be able to transfer cryptocurrencies contained in that wallet without permission. In short, Gemini's security protocols are no second to anyone and the possibilities that funds are stolen are extremely low. Even if such a violation occurs, all the funds are insured by AON and any losses would be offset.

Higher security systems

In addition to the safety of Gemini, Blockfi uses a range of features to keep the accounts of its customers safe. Two-factor authentication is active and all passwords, personal and sensitive information is encrypted. The platform also allows users to practice the "AllowListing" (otherwise known as Whitelisting) on their accounts, so the funds can be collected only to certain addresses, that needs to be specified and approved.

It would take an immensely sophisticated attack to extract funds from Blockfi and even in that case the insurance would cover any loss. No customer deposit has been stolen and if an account is compromised, it would be immediately frozen for a week and a video conferencing would be conducted with the customer concerned to confirm its identity. You can then run the steps to change passwords and email addresses to ensure that the customer can resume control of your personal account.

Institutional Blockfi services

Blockfi provides institutional services such as personalized loans also in the form of stablecoins, cryptocurrency and fiat currencies such as USD. Blockfi supports quick onboarding i.e. a rapid execution of exchanges with its company level reporting. You will be followed step by step in the entire loan creation process. For more details, you can contact the team by filling out a special request form provided by the site.

In the arena of cryptocurrency-based loans and encryption accounts, Blockfi is certainly well positioned among the first 3 platforms available in the market. The platform constantly innovates and always adds new features. Considering the high interest rate it offers right now and the fact that it has been in business for over 4 years, we can advise you to put a portion of your holdings into a Blockfi interest account.

<u>Conclusion</u>

Congratulations on making it to the end of this book, we hope you found some useful insights to take your cryptocurrency trading skills to the next level. As you should know by now, the world of Bitcoin is extremely complicated and there is a new "opportunity" every way you look. However, our experience tells us that only by taking things seriously and having a proper plan you can develop your investing skills to the point that you can actually accumulate wealth.

Our final advice is to stay away from the shining objects that the world of cryptocurrencies offers you every day. Simply dollar cost average into Bitcoin and study the world of cryptocurrencies in depth. After you have sufficient knowledge on what you are talking about, you can go ahead and invest into other cryptocurrencies. Analyze your results, improve your money management skills and become the master of your emotions.

As you can see, there are no shortcuts you can take. Easy money does not exist. What exists is the possibility to start from zero and work your way up to become a professional Bitcoin investor. The journey might be difficult, but it is certainly worth it.

CPSIA information can be obtained
at www.ICGtesting.com
Printed in the USA
BVHW031429140521
607266BV00001B/57

9 781802 661958